WHERE THE RUBBER MEETS THE ROAD

A Christian Book for Unbelievers

Acknowledgements

My dearest daughters Tracy and Brogan my son Barclay and grandson Dylan

To my Ma and Da for being there all the time

To all my family, especially Alexander
and the staff who cared for him, at Spinal Injuries, Southern General Hospital, Glasgow

Thanks to

Pastor Alex Gillies for his perpetual encouragement

Not forgetting everyone at AOG Govan Victory

Credits

The Author and Publisher have made every effort to trace the ownership of all quotes and photographs in this book. In the event of any question that may arise from the use of any quote or photograph, we regret any error made and will be pleased to make the necessary correction in any future editions of this book.

Bible Translation:	God's Word, unless otherwise stated
Vine's:	*Vine's Expository Dictionary of Bible Words*
United Christian Broadcasters Ltd.: PO Box 255, Stoke on Trent ST4 8YY	*The Word For To-Day* their FREE inspirational booklets
Care: 53 Romney Street London SW1P 3RF	The vision of Care is of a praying church, interceding on a wide range of issues. To this end the daily prayers are now available on email, to subscribe log on to **www.care.org.uk/prayer/diary** or email **prayer@care.org.uk**
Phillips:	*Great Thoughts Funny Sayings*

Addison Wesley Longman: One Jacob Way, Reading, MA 01867-3999

Perseus Books Group: 10 East 53rd Street, New York 10022.

Pearson Education: Edinburgh Gate, Harlow, Essex CM20 2JE

Image Reproduction Credits

© Glasgow Museums: The St Mungo Museum of Religious Life & Art	*Christ of St John of the Cross* Salvador Dali
Eastman Kodak Company:	*The Joy of Photography* photographs reprinted courtesy of Eastman Kodak Company. KODAK is a trade mark. © Photographic Credits as follows:

	Page				
	Number	John Paul Murphy	35	Ansel Adams	65
		Neil Montanus	42	George Silk	68
Craig Stewart	6	Trey Morgan	46	Alvin Cohen	70
Janet Tait	8	Robert Bastard	48	George Ingram	72
Edward Murphy	22	Ralph Cowan	51	Brian Brake Photo	79
Peter Gails	26	Ryszard Horowitz	58	Researchers Inc.	

WHERE THE RUBBER MEETS THE ROAD

A Christian Book
for Unbelievers

A Life of Rhyme

Pat Clark

ISBN 0 9543345 0 7

Published by
Garthland Print limited,
Glasgow

Printed by
Garthland Design & Print,
Glasgow

Contents

Matthew 10v32

"" If you confess me before men,
I will confess you before my Father ""

Jesus

INTRODUCTION

HOW'S YOUR LIFE AS A CHRISTIAN ?

1. Do you have a perfect relationship with our God and heavenly Father? Allowing the Holy Spirit to fill and direct the paths you walk as you worship our Saviour Jesus?

2. Are you having an ongoing exquisite relationship with your wife/husband/partner/parent that has an idyllic reaction on adoring children/friends who show you total love and respect?

3. Are you the light at your place of employment/learning and enjoying your work mates/classmates friendship and seeing them copy the example you show?

4. Are you keeping sin at bay?

   If you have managed to answer yes to all four points above, then it is time for you to celebrate, as you've obviously been raptured.

You have probably heard the story about the new Christian who parachuted out of a plane into the Indian jungle. The cords from the chute got caught in the trees and he was left hanging with his feet six inches from the ground. To his horror, from the rustle in the trees came a large hungry male tiger. He thought "O Lord, at least let this be a Christian tiger." The tiger walked around him a couple of times, smelling and sizing up the young man. It then knelt down on it's back legs, put it's two large paws together and said "For what I am about to receive I am truly thankful."

While our Lord has plans to prosper us and not to harm us, we need to understand that He knows what He is doing in our lives. We do tend to forget that there can be and is a baptism of suffering. Sometimes we don't listen and Father does know how we should learn. It is usually in the "University of the World" that we mature. The reality of a Christian's expectations and his walk often don't go in the same direction. In my walk with our Lord and God I have found that trials are a way of life in the walk I take.

I am so grateful for a few scriptures (below) that allow me to know that He understands how I often do not meet the mark. It also allows me to see that sometimes it takes the heat of the crucible to unlodge the deep things of the heart.

John 16v33
I've told you this so that my peace may be with you. In the world you will have trouble.
But cheer up I have overcome the world.

James 1v2-3
My brothers and sisters, be very happy when you are tested in different ways. You know that such testing of your faith produces endurance. Endure till your testing is over. Then you will be mature and complete, and you won't need anything.

Romans 8v28
We know ALL THINGS work together for the good of those who love God - those whom He has called according to His plan.

What I would like to express is that sometimes it is hard to walk the walk. Hopefully this wee book of poems (and things) will allow you to see *Where the Rubber Meets the Road*. At the end of it all our Glorious Father waits for the restoration of His children.

It may sound strange but I have always known the presence of God in my life. As far back as I can remember I have been aware that He was a living force in my being. Even as a baby at a year old in hospital, I knew of His presence. My mother was and still is God conscious. She and her four sisters and brother were abandoned by their mother when she was fourteen. The family was brought up in a convent, where my ma's faith was sharpened and strengthened by a God who cared for her in her loneliness.

 Let me put the record straight, while I've always known about the Lord's presence I never gave Him access into my being till I was thirty three years old. In March 83 I gave Him my life not because I wanted to (although I did) but because I had to. Up until this point I had crammed so much garbage into my existence that I felt I was on a never ending, revolving wheel, that refused to stop.

At the time I suppose in the world's eyes you could say I was comfortable. Self-employed as a car dealer and owning my own home I did not have any financial worries. The turmoil that was going on in my mind was coming from the garbage and life-style I had embarked on from a youth.

At nine years old I was put in Larchgrove Remand Home. On the 7th Nov 1961 (11 years old) I graduated to St. Joseph's approved school, in Tranent Edinburgh, to be quickly followed by a spell in St. Mary's approved school in Bishopbriggs. I made it big time when I was sentenced to Polmont borstal at sixteen years of age. My incarceration career continued in Barlinnie's Young Offenders E Hall. This was followed by a few sentences in Barlinnie itself. The last sentence being eighteen months.

 I remember, while in Barlinnie (I was 25), saying to myself, "By the time I am thirty three I am going to have made it." I was aware that Our Lord Jesus Christ had fulfiled His earthly purpo e at that age but I was saying it for my own human benefit. I believe He heard it in another way. I always prayed in institutions but these prayers were repetitious and only helped me to keep my mind off other things or until I fell asleep.

I had many good friends who started to get into dope and I must admit it was funny the things they got up to. Even though these pals were addicted I managed to keep clear of drug abuse until I was twenty nine years old. When I took my first joint I was one of those who went in deep. Within the next four years I had been hospitalised with *Hepatitis (It was called non A non B in those days) twice through sharing needles with other addicts. What I can say about this period is that I managed to keep my business going (as well as using drugs) due to two factors. First of all I had friends who were drug dealers, so my drugs cost nothing or were cheap. Secondly I was a workaholic, so missing a shift was sacrilege.

 At thirty two I spent sixteen weeks in Barlinnie C Hall (remand) charged with being in possession of 15 kilos of cannabis. While I was legally innocent of the charges, my previous convictions and circumstantial evidence, were going to assure me of an eight year prison sentence (according to my lawyer and QC). To cut a long story short, the charges were dropped and I walked free from court (August 82). But I was not a happy man. I had vengeance in my heart against one of my **co-accused who was sentenced to five years. It was then I started to plan revenge and retaliation on the day he would be released from prison. Father had other ideas.

I could not carry the weight of hatred or problems from worldly burdens any longer. So on a dark December night, kneeling in a very cold room, I asked Jesus into my life. It's where He wanted to be from the very beginning but He waited all those years until I invited Him in. It took another three months for me to be drawn to the church at New Life Christian Centre in Drumchapel. On the first night I visited I was baptised in the Holy Spirit and spent the next ten years there.

So why a book of poems an' things? Well I don't know why I got the revelation of God in the way that I did. What I do know is that Jesus is very real to me. I know how it feels to be redeemed and cleaned by His sacrifice. I am not ashamed of Him nor His gospel. I have seen and heard people who get embarrassed at the mention of His word or even His name. I used to be one of those people and yet I was totally aware of God, but not prepared to let Him sit on the seat of my heart. I was held back by what man thought of me. So hopefully this wee book will let people see that I was a man who thought he knew 'Where The Rubber Met the Road'. In a worldly sense I probably did, but adding His presence into my life gives me the balance I need as a human being. If one poem or comment touches a heart and directs it on to the Saviour's path then I will be blessed.

Another thing I would like to say is that every one of us has faults, failings and weaknesses. That includes our churches our leaders, our intentions and our actions. That encourages me so much because Paul informs us in:

2Cor.12v8
I begged the Lord three times to take it away from me. But He told me; "My kindness is all you need. My power is strongest when you are weak." So I will brag even more about my weaknesses in order that Christ's power will live in me.

What Paul is saying is that when I am at my weakest points in life He is at His strongest. Feelings might try and tell you otherwise, but be patient and let His Power come through. It's then we become strong because the power of the Lord starts to operate. It lets me see that my faults and failings can be overcome in Him. It's not unholy to feel rotten or inadequate but it can take time and testing to turn our weaknesses over to Him. (He wants to be invited in to our problems as well as our hearts.)

"Where the rubber met the road" was where Jesus was and still is to this day. So I pray this wee book is an encouragement to you, not with airy fairy spiritual stories nor with religious piety but with a power that is real. Sometimes it's hard being a Christian, sometimes we can't feel the blessing, sometimes the prosperity isn't there. That doesn't mean Father doesn't love us. It just means that His timing and our timing can be different. Let's wait and see, you know He will come good.

*Hepatitis

A few years ago the friend who had caught Hepatitis at the same time as me phoned to tell me that I needed to go and get a check up. Apparently the Hepatitis I had (non A, non B) was now called Hepatitis C. He had had tests done and they came back positive. We both had been infected together with the virus all those years ago.

While I knew in my heart of hearts that I was cleansed from my past I felt a wee twinge of apprehension when I went for the test. The results came back negative. The doctor said that I was clear and although that it was not rare, it seldom happens. He said he knew I had once been infected with Hepatitis C because I had antibodies in my blood, but there was now no sign of the disease.

**Co-accused

If my co-accused had pled guilty in the first place then the anxiety I experienced and the time I spent in prison would have been less. Our friendship was over as he refused to take the "RAP" thus prolonging a nightmare. The month he was released from prison I visited him at his garage and asked him to forgive me for the hatred and venom I had shown towards him. I was speaking to him only a couple of months ago and only felt friendship and love towards him.

FACTS THOUGHTS AND THEORIES

On November 1st 99 THE WORD FOR TODAY *daily devotions booklet, published this little gem of an article. It refers to Charles Darwin and the "theory".

God used Lady Hope, wife of the senior admiral of the British fleet, to reach Charles Darwin with the gospel during the last years of his life. He was bedridden and she'd often visit him. One afternoon as he was reading his bible, she asked, "What are you studying now?" "Still Hebrews," he replied. "I call it the Royal Book. Isn't it grand?" When she mentioned how popular his theory of evolution had become, he gave her an anguished look and said, "I was a young man then, with un-formed ideas. I thought out queries and suggestions, wondering all the time. . and to my astonishment, those ideas took like wildfire. People made a religion out of them."

Later, Darwin asked Lady Hope if she'd share the word of God with some of his friends in the garden summerhouse. She asked, "What shall I share about?" He replied, "Jesus Christ and His salvation. Is that not the best theme?" Dr. Victor Pearce, an Oxford scholar, says, "When someone tells you evolution explains everything, tell them Darwin discovered a better theme - Jesus Christ and His salvation. If they still doubt, invite them to read his favourite book, which says, "In these last days (God) has spoken to us by his Son. . . through whom He made the universe." (Heb 1v2). The greatest discovery Darwin ever made was finding Jesus as his Saviour. How about you?

*THE WORD FOR TO-DAY.
Free booklets available from; United Christian Broadcasters Ltd, PO Box 255, Stoke on Trent ST4 8YY

THE MANUFACTURER

There is nothing or no one on earth that can understand the heart of man. If you have a car and it breaks down you need the makers advice. Do you need an emergency call out? Do you need a spare part or a service? You might need an overhaul, or even a replacement engine. The body work may not be up to standard. Perhaps you need an MOT. Don't stand at the road side hoping someone will stop with the right part. The Lord has a Freephone facility that is on call 24 hours per day. We have not evolved we have been created. So allow the creator to comfort and adjust you by giving Him access into your heart. Allow Him to give you a daily service by calling on him each morning. He knows how you were made.

Isaiah 44v2
The Lord made you, formed you in the womb, and will help you.

CREATOR

How far can we really sink in grief or on past deeds done
No peace, no rest, no sanctuary nor love from anyone
Where on earth do we turn to, to seek comfort for the heart
Is there anyone out there with a healing hand to impart

There are things said even though we don't fully understand
Firing pain like an arrow with a comment out of hand
Insensitive to one another while sorrow can't be consoled
It's then we realise our being in the heart needs to unfold

We get the love from our children and respect from a friend
But they think we are doing fine and the best they intend
So who can see the heart within, that needs comfort, direction and peace
Is there a man or woman who holds a key bringing that release

I suppose it's time we need to look into a whole new realm
Hoping to find someone close who has both hands on the helm
Perhaps we need to see past the physical, into the spiritual,
which by far is the greater
And return all we have and need, back to Him who is the Creator

BOOK'S ABOUT LIFE'S PATHS

LIFE'S PATHS FROM A BOOK

During my walk as a Christian the Lord has spoken to me directly on several occasions. While our Lord directs us on a daily basis (His word, circumstances, events etc.) sometimes He does speak to us directly. When He has spoken to me it sounds like my own voice but it is so soft and gentle. It has an authority that can only be spiritual. Lying in bed (1983) on the night I gave Him my heart His voice stunned me when He said "If you are speaking to me then get on your knees." So for the second time that night I repented and turned my life over to Him. The voice was so still but it had the effect of reaching right down into my being. Each time I have heard the Lord it has been more powerful and direct than anything taught or spoken from any preacher or teacher of the Word.

Anyway, this was a word spoken to me and for me by the Lord on April 5th 1999. It came at a time when I was at a low ebb needing the reassurance and comfort it brought.

1Kings 19v12
After the earthquake there was a fire,
But the Lord wasn't in the fire. And
after the fire there was a quiet,
whispering voice.

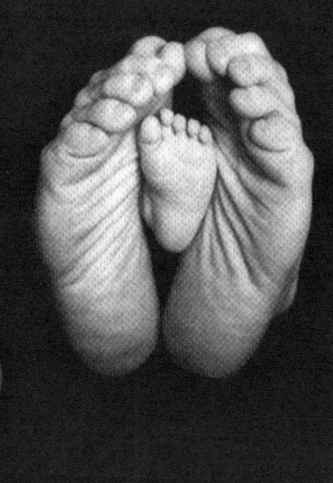

HEAR TO-DAY DOING TO-MORROW

What is whispered can reach the innermost of places. While shouting can fall on deaf ears.

Church Tales

Giving a prophetic word from the Lord to the congregation, the orator "burped" then said,
"Pardon me my people."

FATHER'S WORD

Come this way and let me enter your heart by way of your ears

Let me saturate you with my presence, consoling any doubt pain or fears

Allow my Spirit to move with the intentions to love comfort and protect

Keeping back condemnation and oppression your enemy tries to infect

For I am the Lord God Almighty the Father of your spirit and soul

My Agape love for you is eternal as I move to make you whole

My compassion for you is real, when I see you stagger stumble or fall

It's at times like these that you hear me clearly as to your being I call

You know my beloved Son and all the pain and suffering He endured

Sealing up my love on a cross, eternal fellowship is ensured

Now He sits at my right hand as angels bow with praises pure

He completed my eternal plan, your position in this family is sure

For I have set aside a place prepared especially for you

Give your heart and life to me Your Father, who is all knowing all loving and true

I look to that day when we shall be together as one

I with you, you with Me and being pleased at the worship you give my Son

We get daily newspapers every morning that have a shelf life of twenty four hours. It may be the sports section or the political aspect that grabs your attention, but after reading it, it is done. We may have some comment to make during the day about an article that caught our attention. Or we might even have another wee glance through the paper, browsing at the snippets we missed. In general it is binned, it is finished until the next day when a brand new one is purchased.

Luke 11v3-4   NIV
Give us each day our daily bread.
Forgive us our sins, (daily?) for we also forgive
everyone who sins against us (daily?).
And lead us not into temptation (daily?).

So it is with blessings. Let us ask and receive from a God who is daily renewing.

Ps. 68v19 KJ
Blessed be the Lord, who daily loadeth us
with benefits, even the God of our salvation.

Church Tales

There was a Saturday night dance at a local church. A good time was had by one and all. The next morning during the service one of the congregation stood up to give an enthusiastic word from the Lord. "My children," he said "I was in your midst when you danced last night, I was there as you enjoyed fellowshiping with one another. In fact I have not had such a good time since I parted the Red Sea, sayeth the Lord."

(Daily) BLESSINGS ON YOU

I pray for prosperity in all things you do

I pray for comfort, when hard times you see through

I pray for direction in any mundane walk

I pray for wisdom, when you take breath to talk

I pray for clarity at times you choose and pick

I pray for healing, when you're down or sick

I pray for peace when problems abound

I pray for a circle of angels, as they gather around

I pray for transparency in all things unclear

I pray for patience, for solutions that are not near

I pray for freedom when addiction pulls the reigns

I pray for a sound mind, free from mind bending games

I pray for abundance in times of dryness and drought

I pray for faith, at times when you may doubt

I pray for conviction, the type that cleans the soul

I pray for vision as you walk on the path of your goal

I pray that you become a blessing to all those around

I pray that you excel in any instrument, or verbal sound

I pray for your children, in God they will seek

I pray for you every day, covering all the week

I pray for your relationship with partner, parent or child

I pray for perseverance, in circumstances that grow wild

I pray for your spirit when the flesh tries to retaliate and kick

I pray your prayers are answered, ever so quick

I pray you are consoled in times of grief

I pray the Lord collects every tear, giving you relief

I pray for endurance in any times of testing

I pray for comfort, when you are asleep or resting

I pray for release in times when you falter

I pray for persistence, for the things you want to alter

I pray for company when loneliness bites deep

I pray for your soul into which the Holy Spirit would seep

I pray for a softening in the heart that is set

I pray for the desires of that same heart to be met

I pray for surety when compromise attacks

I pray for your gelling, in all of God's facts

I pray for revelation when with praises you sing

I pray for you all gifts, from the living King

I pray He pours on you more blessing than you can hold

I pray your joy explodes as you are gathered into His fold

I pray for Father's grace to cover you like a stream

I pray for you to be yourself, you'll know what I mean

Situations can arise in our lives that causes a change in our attitude, lifestyle, perception etc. Depending on the experience, our lives are NEVER THE SAME AGAIN. The change can work both ways good or bad but we always seem to adapt to the new circumstances. So it is with Father, when He touches our lives, we are never the same again.

I have the most wonderful son (Barclay) who lightens my life beyond the words I could put on this paper. He is a bit of a lad to say the least. Four years before he was born, the Lord told me in prayer that we were going to have a "Special Son". I took this in my stride and told everybody and anybody that wanted to hear about our new son who was on the way. We even picked his name. After a while nothing seemed to be happening regarding a pregnancy. After we both went for tests we were told that my wife had a gynaecological problem and a baby was out of the question. In fact her doctor recommended that she should have a hysterectomy.

We refused this option. A young lady surgeon offered us micro surgery but promised nothing. After the operation and a weeks rest in hospital, my wife was allowed home. A couple of months later we sat in front of the surgeon to be told that my wife's fallopian tubes were too far gone. We thanked the doctor very much but informed her that we believed God rather than the tests. As we walked from the hospital we didn't know that my wife was a month pregnant with Barclay.

At his birth, all the staff in the labour room left us alone almost as soon as he was born. (While they knew Barclay had Down's Syndrome they were not allowed to tell us. Apparently that has to be done by a pediatrician and there was none working that night). In the labour room I lifted my son up above my head and thanked Father for this gift. We dedicated him to the Lord and thanked Him for allowing us to bring up "This wee miracle".

I drove home (it was more like floating) with a smile as long as a mile. Listening to the radio and hearing the football team I supported being put out of a European competition (even though our centre had scored four goals) meant not a jot. This was real life. This was joy. This was fulfilment. I then knew what blessings really were.

I was called back to the hospital later (11pm) that night to be told that Barclay had Down's Syndrome. The drive home was very different to the one I had a couple of hours earlier. Hot tears burned my face and I heard myself saying aloud to the Lord "You said he was going to be special". The Lord spoke very gently to me when He said "The other children are normal, this one is special". After the few days Barclay spent in intensive care we had him home. He has been through all sorts of major operations and discomforts since then but above all else he loves music and a good praise time to the Lord suits him fine.

The inspiration for the song (Never The Same Again) came from a relative who found it hard to understand that two Christian parents who had decided to follow the Lord, had given birth to a child with Down's. I took it on board and asked the Lord if it had anything to do with my past or was it something passed down through our genes. (In the bible it says curses). I really couldn't care tuppence as to why Barclay had Down's but I was interested what the Lord had to say, more for the sake of the relatives than my own. He turned me to the blind man in the chapter of **John 9** and I got my full answer in verse **3**:

> *"Neither this man nor his parents sinned"* said Jesus
> *"but this happened so that the work of God might be
> displayed in his life."*

I'm not super spiritual about it but it is a joy to see my wee boy make the progress he has made. Just like any child he can also be the cheekiest boy in his class. In any event we have never been the same since he was born. So first I give you the poem followed by the song.

BARCLAY

Barclay is the **name** of a boy without **fame** who in prayer is a promise come *true*
The dearest **son** with much **fun** in a family he loves through and *through*
Shaking his **head** the expert **said** to us childbirth was not an *option*
All they could **say** was a hysterectomy **today** and perhaps try for a*doption*

No physical **doubt** at the prophesy handed **out** we gave our baby a *name*
No worry or **fear** nor the odd salty **tear** when the final test *came*
Four years to **wait** for the promise to **relate** even when doctors said " *No* "
After the **tests** and hospital **rests** in the womb he started to *grow*

It was pleasure and **joy** at the birth of a **boy** the beginning of a life brand *new*
Not just a **baby** nor hope and **maybe** but God's word had come *through*
I was **contented** and firmly **cemented** knowing Father was on my *side*
Gratitude was longer than **latitude** and the over flow I could not *hide*

The 27th of **September** in 89 I **remember** the night he was born so *well*
Parkhead was **filling** and people were **milling** as the crowd started to *swell*
7.20 pm into the world he **shot** with the ear he **got** turned down and stuck at the *top*
Jakinofski scored **four** I danced on the **floor** not caring if it was in Ibrox or the *Kop*

The room was **vacated** by staff not **related** expressing the hospitals maternity *code*
Wrapped in a **sheet** I could see his **feet** as I held him up to Father in dedication *mode*
I didn't **know** as he started to **grow** about the problems that bring sighs and *frowns*
Called back at **night** with no one in **sight** I was told my baby had a syndrome called *Down's*

Left alone to make my way **home** I drove with a heavy *heart*
Tears fell **free** as I struggled to **see** yet knowing that my God was still a *part*
"Special" He **said** were the words in my **head** I remembered Father's promise to *me*
"I will not **deny**" came the soft **reply**, "He is special, have patience, wait and **see**"

Days went **past** as time does not **last** I would sneak in to visit intensive *care*
I'd **touch** and talk as **much** but leaving was hard from my son to *tare*
It seems so **strange** trying to **rearrange** how my concern was about future *plans*
Worry about **this** or things **amiss** but was it not God who placed him into my *hands*

To and **fro** with places to **go** we got him home to his new family *cot*
Seeing him **eat** was really **neat** and the anxieties of the day came to *naught*
Right from the **start** we were never **apart** especially at a want or a *need*
His speech is a bit **slow** but he knows where to **go** when it's time for fun or a *feed*

He's had many an **operation** with full **co-operation** from doctors and nurses *alike*
Tummy heart and **hips** they can't stop his **lips** from telling them to get on their *bike*
He loves our **Lord,** the Trinity, **God** and followers who call Jesus their *own*
In his own **way** he's here to **stay**, as he witnesses with seeds that are purely *sown*

He plays the **guitar** with melody from **afar** and he does know how to *praise*
He gets the tea **ready** when hips are not **steady** for a house group he wants to *raise*
Just like any other wee **boy** he plays with a **toy** but one thing for which I am *ecstatic*
Fathers given a **son** who is much **fun** even though his behaviour is sometimes *erratic*

So what can I **say** about the blessings of the **day** do you need me to go on any *more*
The fulfilment I **get** with problems I've **met** even though at the time they seem *sore*
It has all come to **pass** whether you're a boy or a **lass** your pathway in this life is *set*
You can walk **it** or you can talk **it** or turn it over to the Saviour I have *met*

COINCIDENTAL MIRACLES

Care Christian Action Research & Education are a group who send out prayer sheets for intercessory prayer. These sheets give 13 weekly topics over 92 days spanning all sorts of criteria.

> *Barclay was eight months old when he had to go through open heart surgery. Even trusting in the Lord we were anxious to say the least. A friend gave me a used sheet from Care which had the 92 separate topics.*

As we stood in the hospital that morning I read from a used stained prayer list the forth last prayer from the three month cycle. It read-:

Wed 6th June 1990   *Intercede against the mentality which favours eradicating certain diseases by ante-natal screening and then abortion. Pray that we would learn to value people with Down's syndrome.*

You can imagine how humble I felt. The Creator of the universe had been hearing prayer from people all over Britain. He was listening to prayer He had placed on someone else's heart in the first place. Neat.

On seeing Barclay's surgeon I was so high I started to blab all that the Lord had done for us. The doctor only wanted to explain the procedure for the operation that was about to take place. I felt I had to stop rambling as I did not want to unnerve the man who was going to have my son's life in his hands.

He just smiled and said "Mr Clark I am a Christian and lay preacher. My staff and I have a prayer time before we start every operation."

For information Log on to: www.care.org.uk/prayer/diary or email prayer@care.org.uk

never the same again

(John 9)

a father looks and cries
mother dear our babies eyes
understanding a child's plight
that's been born without sight
brings pain tears and grief
to which there's no relief

chorus (parents)

there's no freedom no freedom from the pain
and we'll never be the same again
we'll never be the same again
oh no we'll never be the same again
never the same again

only begging left to live
not seeing faces that give
condemned to darkness it seems
no hope ambition or dreams
no wife no children to embrace
realisation to be faced
all they can do now is pray
that his sight will come one day

chorus (parents)

rabbi is it sin that blinds, he hears a voice say clear
neither this man or his parents caused the blindness
nor the fear
no, it was for father's glory
so you can tell the story
about the power you now see
on a blind man set free

chorus (jesus)
i give freedom etc.

hands now pick him up, on his eyes he feels the mud
he hears that voice again , like the force of a flood
"go wash in the silom pool giving glory to god's rule"
wash, wash wash away, wash wash wash away the mud

chorus (jesus)
i give freedom etc.

as the light poured in
out went darkness pain and sin
it's now i look and see
at the face that released me
do you believe in the son
yes my lord you are the one
and i bow, bow bow down, yes i bow, bow bow down

chorus (blind man)
i got freedom etc.

called in by the sanhedrin
where has you blind son been
don't ask us ask him
he now sees and it wasn't our sin

chorus (parents)
we got freedom etc.

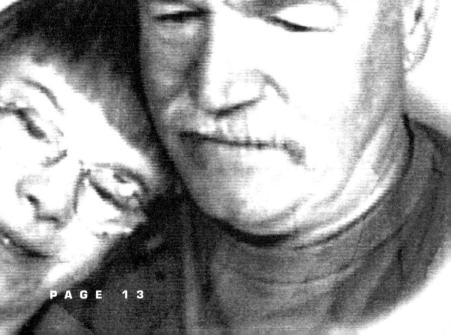

Exod. 20v3
Thou shalt have no other Gods before me KJ

Jesus said in John 15v13
Greater love has no-one than this, that he lay down his life for his friends.

Genesis 2v18
Then the Lord God said, It is not good for man to be alone.
I will make a helper who is right for him.

The above scriptures gives man priorities about his life with God and with his fellow man. *A Man's Way With a Woman* is probably as high up in the emotional and commitment stakes as it gets.

I actually changed the name of this poem from **"A Man's Way With a Woman"** to **"A Man's God"**. I then went on and watered down the poem to make it kind of spiritual. I suppose I was just embarrassed as my upbringing tended to leave a sort of stain in my mind when it came to anything sexual or sensual. Dirty books and dirty talk were my introduction to the sweetest gift Father has given to a man and a woman. The enemy of man, satan, has another name for this communion. It's the distortion called lust. He arouses love before it so desires.

The thought of being able to express love for a woman made me feel too human. Alas that is what I am and that is the way my Lord made me. Being divorced also made me feel I had no right to express myself in words. Anyway I give you the poem in it's entirety.

I remember reading Song of Songs for the first time and thought that it was a bit strong and must be a story comparing Gods intimacy with man. It's not (Although many comparisons can and have been done). No matter how hard we look in this book our Creator has given us an intimate communion as human beings. Its a human communion between man and woman blessed and ordained by God. The third chapter in Song of Songs is quite clear of the love the beloved has for the one she seeks but in:

Sol. 3v5 She says:
Do not arouse or awaken love until it so desires*

*LET LOVE SLEEP

If love is so wonderful, as this poem (in Song of Songs) so beautifully sings, shouldn't people pursue it recklessly? Yet the beloved warns them not to. Three times she urges others not to force love, but to let it develop at it's own rate. Love should wait for it's own time. *NIV Insight Bible

Sol. 8v7
Raging waters cannot extinguish love and rivers will never wash it away

Eph. 5v30-31 (Genesis 2v24)
We are parts of His (Jesus)body. That is why a man will leave his father and mother and be united with his wife, and the two will be one. This is a great mystery (I'm talking about Christ's relationship to the church). While Paul is making the point about Jesus the comparison is there regarding a man and woman in wedlock.

A Man's Way With A Woman

What can be said when all has been spoken
What is there to mend when nothing is broken

What tune can be played, as melody comes from you
What heaviness can stand straight when your presence walks through

What beat does not quicken when with a sparkle your eyes gaze
What true perfection you bring as in my arms you laze

Oh how I love to stand and protect you true and strong
I look to your wisdom and beauty as in gentleness we go along

Then you lift me as I watch your laughing smile unfold
Contentment is fulfiled that lets me feel my heart's heart is sold

What about a man's way with a woman, that's only one side of the story
What about the completeness I feel when you become a part of my glory

What about your mind with my mind as we open up to correction
What about your body to my body when we fit in intimate perfection

Is not the breadth and depth of our love a mystery indeed
I give to you, you give to me, your person I desire and want to feed

So what can be uttered in words as I now come to finish
What can be said of love intense as an eternal state, never to diminish

What then my dearest woman when I see your being and your fun
What then as with holy scripture Father said " Two shall become One "

LONG LIFE BATTERY
Naturally women live longer than men - look how long they remain girls.

TRINITY THOUGHTS

Oh how we like to dwell on good things and memories of the past
Nostalgic reminiscence fills us with warmth like summer rays in a sunset cast
We pick and select chosen times of comfortable grandeur tied to personal feats
Coupled with romantic fulfilment, births, and of course opponents defeats

So let us take stock and see man's original war now finished and done
For it is time to rejoice and know a victory at the beginning of time was won
At the fall the keys of man were surrendered to a serpent with a counterfeit deal
But words spoken promised that a head would be crushed by the crucified heel

For our foe an everlasting pit has been carved out with no bottom in sight
No matter how much he tries to lie, nor no matter how much he tries to fight
The angelic hosts who sing to our God with eternal praises in their hearts
Live to serve and minister before the ancient satanic enemy departs

Creation waited in expectation as the Prince of Peace was revealed
Fulfiling Father's promise that through Him a covenant would be sealed
He lived the sorrow and felt the pain as He walked the chosen path
Giving up His spirit and crying to Father, he felt Adam's separation wrath

Oh the majesty and glory of one so tortured and drained of His lifes blood
Meant that the action of this man would turn the fall into a salvation flood
Putting on His yoke for our burdens and receiving a healing balm for our pain
Means millions have turned to the spotless Lamb who was crucified and slain

Does not your spirit leap at the love and commitment He continually shows
Totally expressing Father's will in everything He does and every where He goes
The most Holy Spirit who dwells in man is a deposit that He is alive and well
Oh, open your heart and feel the peace, that prompts us to testify and tell

For no eye has seen and no ear has heard and no mind can conceive
The plans He has for us and they start at the time from when we receive
Ah, the Trinity God so much a Oneness and yet so easy to feel the three
The covenant was united and recorded to bring release to you and me

ECLECTIC LESSON

"I can't let this go to print. I don't wish to embarrass you." As a professional, Ian Wright (Publisher) felt that the inconsistencies were too numerous to allow us to go onto the production of this book. Two proof readings had not cleared the errors and mistakes.

In the synopsis on the back of the book, for which I am grateful, Ian mentions, "THIS ECLECTIC BOOK". At first I thought it was something I caught, but when I looked it up, it was spot on.

ENGLISH DICTIONARY: Eclectic: selecting what seems best from various styles, doctrines, ideas, methods etc.

So I must have been an "Eclectic Maniac" all of my life before I met Jesus. Do you know anybody like that?

When I was given the first proof of my writings, it looked so good in book form, I was delighted. Now, when I look at that first book, marked and scored with pen and coloured inks, pointing out errors and mistakes, I think of the life that I used to lead. At the time I thought my life was fine, but on inspection I came up short, far short.

The finished book is a joy and gives me personal satisfaction, but to my little girl Brogan it is a threat. She asked me if she would still be able to see me if the book made me famous. The lessons I took from the above events are profound.

In between getting the first book from the printers, and seeing the finished product, I was given a perfectly blank white duplicate book. There was no mistakes or errors in the book. Everything was spotless, even on close inspection. This allowed me to inspect the proposed quality and texture of cover and paper. The paper the publisher chose was one that inks, from producing the book, would not rub on to the opposing pages.

Can I honestly say that my favourite book is the blank one. It shows me what Jesus did for me. He erased all the blemishes and stains of my former life. He washed away all the ink and colour stain from an existence that looked okay to me at the time. The blank book also allows me to give Him the glory, because I don't want the hassle of thinking I did this myself. I do not want any of the complete books (old or new) to rub onto the blank spotless one. Because on the original book there is stain and sin and on the completed new book, pride awaits to get a mention on the blank spotless pages.

He is my Lord and this book is not designed for me to tell you how much I know about God. It is designed to let us know how much He knows and loves us. If what I believe is true then Father will touch you sometime during the reading of this book, for that is my prayer. I can't touch your spirit with photos or ink, neither with colour nor lyrics. But He (Jesus) can give you a revelation that His love for you is true and eternal.

Being a blank book is wonderful. If you want, Jesus through the Holy Spirit will put clear messages on clean sheets in your clean book, daily. What I would suggest is that beside your blank book you put the Bible. That will allow you to copy things into your life from the book that needs no correction. Just read the small print.

ECLECTIC LESSON

Ah rote a **book**, a long time it **took**, bit finely it's finished an *dun*
A price wiz **goat**, fur the stuff a **rote**, tae allow the presses tae *run*
It's taken a **while**, tae compose it in **style**, patience wiz the *key*
Mha english iz **sad**, bit that's no **bad**, coz fae language purists ah'm *free*

It seemed a good **idea**, joined up wurds tae **steer**, bit grammur an spellin needed *corrected*
Then taken **away**, wae a nod of **dismay**, coz every page, barrin nun, wiz *infected*
Oot this wee **story**, cums a lesson not **phoney**, fae a daughter an a print *boss*
Eclectic he **sed**, wiz a wurd no familure tae mha **hed**, even if ah did feel at a *loss*

Noo getin tae the **crunch**, wae a spiritual **punch**, let me deliver a message minus the *glam*
No jist wan book but **three**, did mha Lord let me **see**, as to wer in God I *am*
The furst wan wiz aw **mine**, wae a mountain tae **refine**, every page hid mistakes *galore*
Next book on **site**, wiz clean and **white**, az it wiz blank showin me the paper in *store*

Wae the thurd and last **complete**, the finishrd edishon iz **neat**, an rests safely in yer *hauns*
Mha wee girl **sed**, the other night in bed, 'Da, wen yer famous wull we still hiv family *bonds*?'
In hur face ah saw **fear**, fae a prowlin giant **near**, the wan of separation called *Pride*
Ah looked at the **furst**, ah looked at the **last**, an decided the book in the middle iz were ah'l *abide*

Ye see ah thote ah wiz **ok**, wen in the wurld ah did **play**, coz ah did wit ah thote tae get *by*
Jist like the furst **print**, even though ah wiz given meny a **hint**, mha sins wur thick and as *high*
The finished **article**, stands withoot a dust **particle**, and may even shine oan a book *shelf*
Bit ah prefer the **blank**, jist in case my ego becomes **frank**, and ah looz wit He gave up fur *myself*

Parents will know of the joy a child can bring. Seeing their character and personality taking shape is a blessing that I fully appreciate. Brogan has serious opposition at home. She has an elder sister who is the mother of her nephew Dylan who is one year older than her. Being a year older, Dylan refuses to give her the "Auntie" respect she feels she is entitled too. She also has opposition from her big brother Barclay. One of the things that impresses me about my daughter is her bravery. Her two male relatives are a lot larger than she is but that does not stop her from pushing her corner right up to the point "Dad" is called in.

Brogan is such a bright wee spark with questions that burst into flames. This poem is a compilation of comments and actions she has participated in.

BROGAN

Let me tell you about my wee lassie Brogan, a princess so funny and *bright*,
In my **presence** she is the **essence** of a heart filled with joy and *delight*,
There's always a **query**, a comment, or **theory**, or an opinion about this and *that*,
Talking about **dogs**, or advert **frogs**, she's also friendly with next door's *cat*.

Her Grandad and **Gran** with love they **scan** even when she becomes a *pain*,
Her friendship with **them** gets full marks of **ten**, its all in their bonding *gain*,
Bigger and **bolder** brother, and nephew **older**, both can give her a hard *time*,
But she doesn't **hide** shrugging them **aside**, I know my wee daughter will be *fine*.

In the morning when **day** is **dawning**, I give her an extra ten minutes to get *up*,
After her **stretch** and Barclay is **fetched**, it's toast with fresh orange juice in her *cup*,
She sits at the **fire** trying to **inspire** Barclay's selection on the tapes video *recorder*,
Most times it's **quiet**, without any **riot**, or without any serious *disorder*.

Brogan **inspects** and often **directs** her plans and purposes for the *day*,
Using Dad, or **Mum**, to incorporate **fun**, being seven is a serious time for *play*,
Options get **shuffled**, without her being **ruffled**, how the grown ups will *feel*,
Then its time to go **biking**, or for **hiking**, or for a quick McDonalds "Happy *Meal*."

Being dressed **first** is almost a **must** never failing to let me *know*,
With anticipating **looks**, she packs her **books**, in a school bag full and ready to *go*,
In times of **gloom**, with impending **doom**, she can sometimes fall into a *mood*,
But with the promise of a **trip**, to straighten her **lip**, her gait changes from bad to *good*.

Both front teeth fell **out**, without any **clout**, but that hasn't altered her *looks*,
So **pretty**, and often **witty**, no change appears till chewing, and with her cheeks, *sooks*,
The idea of a tooth **fairy**, to her wasn't **scary**, it was a wonderland *thrill*,
With all the **money**, it was financially **funny**, her tuck box she could now go and *fill*.

Brogan is so **precious**, with laughter **infectious**, a gem of a jewellers finest *carat*,
Conversations a **joy** with girl or **boy**, she could talk the wings of red African *parrot*,
For one so **petite**, I must **repeat**, that she fills my heart with more than a *sigh*,
Sparkling **eyes**, coupled with cute **sighs**, helps to make her the apple of my *eye*.

CHURCH TALES

MICROBIBLE
An Irish Christian invented a microwave bible.
It allowed you to get an eight hour read in
twenty minutes.

When people give us more credit than we deserve then the excess can inflate the ego. So it is in the spiritual. It is so easy to get caught up in boasting. We can boast without opening our mouths. Even patronising a brother or sister can fall into this category. We also know that getting recognition from our fellow man does not get us any spiritual credits, it only gives us the praise from their mouths. If we have any boasting to do, then let it be in Him.

1 John 2v16 NIV
For everything in the world, the cravings of sinful man, the lust of his eyes and the boasting of what he has and does, comes not from the Father but from the world.

A man is what he appears in God's eyes, and not the slightest bit more.
Francis of Assisi

SOUP OF THE DAY

A boasting lady opened her door to a tramp who was asking for something to eat. "Oh" she said loudly, hoping her neighbours would hear. "Would you like some of yesterdays soup?" The tramp was so pleased and said "Yes please ma'am." The lady looked from side to side, and seeing that no one was there to see or hear, said "Then come back to-morrow."

BOAST

He that boasts of his own knowledge proclaims his ignorance.

BOASTIN

Ah don't ker if yer uprite an strait, or a pure holy Joe
Ah don't ker if ye help the needy, as ye go to an fro
Ah don't ker if ye know aw the good an rite things tae say
An ah don't even ker, if ye go tae yer church every single day

Dae ye let everywan see as ye as ye put yer tithe in the plate
Dae ye cum away wi big prers enabalin yer ego tae inflate
Dae ye dae good deeds tae get man's nod of approval
Or dae ye know its aw aboot a clean heart, an sin's permanint removal

Oh ma brother an sister in Jesus Christ oor Lord
We aw staun convicted as oor flesh recognises not the two edge sword
The carnal man want's tae be known, put oan a pedastil, bowed tae an adored
It's like playin fitba, an gettin worshiped by a fanatical an supportin hoard

Did He no say " Worship the Lord your God and serve only the Father "
It's ment tae be mer of a wan tae wan, wae nae pios points tae gather
Bit if ye think aboot it an knew Jesus wiz in yer corner, jist fur yoo tae defend
Hingin alone oan a cross lookin tae the Creator, Hiz life fur yoo He'd spend

Sum o the things ah rite aboot maybe upset ye, even get oan yer goat
Bit am no sayin who's rite or rang, ahm jist sain we'r aw in the same boat
When dragged up Calvary there wisnay wan clap of approval, nor even a thanks
Yit we act as if we ur dain Him a favour wae oor wee holy deeds an salvation
pranks

He also sade that Hiz Glory wiz tae be shared wae nae created bein
Allowin Love Grace an Mercy tae run free over the sinner, He iz dedicated tae freein
It's the things we dae in the quiet as we look tae the Lord o Hosts
Hiz power pours in abundance when man's no there wae boasts

Being fiftyish (and very active during my youth) I find that my body refuses to act and respond in the way it used to. In fact some of the old football knocks have returned to my being with a vengeance. My body seems to be paying me back for not treating it properly in those early years that I played.

After a heart operation I had time to reflect on my age and my life so far. Football is now out the window (watching only) but other things can be and, by the grace of God, will be fulfiled. Being approximately more than two thirds into this life I can look back and be contented in the fact that I know the Christ and Him slain. So at the end of the day Jesus has paid for the journey we take through life. I am pleased to say that there is a bundle of uncollected tickets for the final destination awaiting on those who apply. They have been paid in full and all you have to do is mention His name (Jesus).

There is an appointed time when there will be a selection and a separation. On that day we will stand before Him.

Matt. 25v32
The people of every nation will be gathered in front of Him. He will separate them as a shepherd separates the sheep from the goats.

Who Cares

Carrington Briggs cared not two figs, whether he lived or died
But when he was dead he sat on his bed, and he cried, and he cried, and he cried.

Spike Milligan

Church Tales

After another of those really good fellowship nights at church. A brother in the Lord who had not made it to the gathering stood at the Sunday morning meeting and said, "My people I know you had a great time last night. I know that relationships were strengthened and friends made. In fact had I been there I would have joined in myself."

DESTINATION

Age moves onward and upward like smoke from a locomotive or a morning mist
Muscles slow down as lungs draw shallow like being pressed by a physical fist
Aches and pains return from endeavours along with deeds and labours of the past
Destination is a real thing as time grabs momentum, moving in fast

What have you crammed into your life of times gone by
Did you manage to complete plans and visions, or are you left with a heart felt sigh
Coming into the final platform it's time to get up and off the train
Were is your human baggage? The joy the love and the pain

The multitude of passengers move to the left, but you walk on being one of the few
Because you know you have an exemption, that will take you straight on, and right through
As the inspector calls for your ticket and accepts you at the gate
Fellow travellers move away, considering their earthly chosen fate

No luggage or burdens abound now, as you show your eternal pass
A card marked in Calvary blood, takes you forward into first class
After being inspected and confirmed in the Lamb's eternal book
"Welcome my true and trusted friend." You gaze into Father's look

So it was worth it, the trials the grief and the pain
All you had was faith in the Saviour, that's God's way for gain
Yes there were many blessings too, with abundance galore
But that was only a fore runner, for what Father has in store

" No more death, no more tears or crying for I am making everything new "
" Write these words I give you for they are trustworthy and true "
" You have completed your journey and you have come to your final place "
" It's now time to start your eternity." Fatherly love spills over with a smile from His face

Dedicated to my Auntie Sadie McAteer.

At the time I wrote this poem the newspapers were full of venom and hate. "Ethnic Cleansing" was the current buzz word. No matter what paper I read, or news I saw on television, it was crammed with war, division and murder.

At this time, had I not been a christian, I don't know how I would have felt. It was as if evil was coming to a crescendo. As a believer I was more than comforted to know that we are in a war, a spiritual war. Our Father is in charge and He has that time and hour set aside for His Son's return. It is a war that has already been won. The Lamb's Book of Life is the Lord's Book of Remembrance.

Rev. 21v27
Nothing unclean, no one who does anything detestable, and no liars will ever enter it (City of God). Only those whose names are written in the lamb's book of life will enter it.

"Yer name isnay in the book, an we don't take nick names, confurmashon names, or aliuses"

THE STING

Feeling low one day I went to a relatives home for some tea and fellowship. My young cousin was so full of zeal he was trying to encourage me with words like, "Don't receive it brother, it's an attack from the enemy," and "Give it to the Lord." His words fell on deaf ears. In fact I was a wee bit annoyed and wanted to tell him I could not switch on and off. He tried to cheer me up by playing some gospel music. Just at that point a wasp stung him on the arm. He let out such a cry of pain that his mum and I jumped. As he danced around the living room we both started to laugh and say to him, "Don't receive it, its an attack from the enemy," and "Give it to the Lord." The three of us laughed the afternoon away and to say I was lifted by the time I left would be an understatement.

Eccl. 7v18 says:
It's good to hold on to the one and not let go of the other, because the one who fears God will be able to avoid both extremes.

What a little gem of a scripture. Unfortunately, if you are like me, you will still be trying to apply these words of wisdom to your life. Just like the event above we can get sore stings from time to time. I am sure the Lord allows us to realise we are **human** beings and not spiritual beings.

THE LAMB'S BOOK OF LIFE

Famine and Pestilence, Poverty and Strife
Man against man with disregard for life
Bombs plus corruption, devastation they cast
Old scores are settled trying to empty the past

Nations in turmoil as children starve and die
"How can there be a God" is man's usual cry
Divorce courts are filling, bitterness to bring
Violence erupts, pouring out death as it's sting

Ethnic cleansing, with the destruction of man
Points to the area of a world-wide satanic plan
Hatred for Father's children, is all the devil knows
But our Lord has a place reserved for these demonic foes

Repaying evil for good, that's a major command
Forgiving and loving our enemies, is the strategy He planned
It's easy to love Father, for in all things He is good
But joined in unity with my brother comes a power not fully understood

When that great and dreadful day is upon us like a thief in the night
Who is going to stand in your corner and defend you with light
Not your money nor your plans, not even your behaviour
There is only one answer to the darkness, A glorious Saviour

Can you understand the words that I write
It's the climax of man in a galactical fight
But there is no need to fear, there is no need to run
For the captain of His army is the Trinities only Son

The light of His love leaves the darkness no where to go
Commitment to man, was the sacrifice from the blood flow
Alone He hung and alone He gave
Obedience to Father, that man's souls He should save

Sometimes it seems too spiritual, in this world full of hate and lust
To turn our lives over to a God, full of love understanding and trust
Things are no different from the day's of Noah and Lot
Only this time He is coming back again to thwart the devil's destruction plot

Isn't it amazing that He died for us once before
Now He's coming back again, this time to give us even more
To the left and to the right will our Father cast His look
Scanning the pages to find our name, written on the Lambs eternal book

I do not know of any other subject or person that gives me more enjoyment than Jesus. When I visited the courts during my chequered life, I would get a deep suppressed feeling in my spirit. When I talk or testify about the Saviour, the feelings are in the same area of my being but this time they are with a joy, an expectation and a revelation. I know it's the Holy Spirits presence. Giving Jesus testimony only happens when the Holy Spirit is involved. One thing I do appreciate from my past is that I cannot separate the Trinity. Father, Son and Holy Spirit are genuinely One to me. I know it is a mystery, but it is only a mystery to those who have not met Him.

Rev 19v10b
Worship God, because the testimony of Jesus is the Spirit of prophesy.

FLY MEN

Two young Christian pilots were flying a two seater aeroplane over the Andes. Looking at the back bulkhead of the plane Pat sees that there is only one parachute.

"Wouldn't it be terrible if we fell out." said Pat. "Don't be daft," replied Michael, "We have been pals for years."

holy spirit

Some people snigger an think yer daft
Wile uthers get the impreshon ye've flipped yer lid or jist plain saft
But how kin ah convey the joy that ah get
Talkin an witnessin tae a persun or stranger ah've jist met

Kin ye explain tae me wit makes me want tae testify an tell
Aboot a Saviour who died an saved me fae an eternity in hell
Shood ah no jist be grateful wit fur me He hiz dun
An be contented tae praise an wurship the Faither's only Son

It seems aw the time ther's jist wan thing goin oan in ma spirit
The force that want's me tae gei it away, hiznae eny limit
He'z a livin God the thurd party o the Holy Trinity
An He hovers everywer espeshaly in mha hart's vacinity

He'z the burning feelin the Cumfurter deep doon within
An He propels me tae let people know aboot lifes original sin
Sure he became mer avalable wen Jesus wiz lifted away
An fur eternity mha plan fur Him iz in mha hart tae stay

A gentle wind a ragin fire He alwayz wants tae be involved
Problems an disasters He cumfurts till they ur resolved
Direcshon an revelashon He never hods anythin back
Keepin me oan a strait line an supplyin me wae gifts thit ah lack

Protecshon an blessins wae joy in the things thit ah dae
Checkin an opperatin convicshon in Hiz ain gentle way
He'z all seein all knowin all luvin, Faithers livin force
He'z the wan that keeps me right when ah draw fae Hiz source

FORCES
There are only two forces in the world, the sword and the spirit.
In the long run the sword will always be conquered by the spirit.
Napoleon Bonaparte

M A

I have always been aware of my Ma's upbringing. I knew how hard it was for her but because I did know, it became a part of me, so it was painless. Recently she had her grand children and great grand children all around her in her house. Now 70 she went on to tell them about the circumstances she and her family found themselves in when she was young. I could hear the heaviness of a guilt that wasn't hers. For the first time I fully realised what she had went through. At fourteen she and her brother and sisters were abandoned by her parents. Her one older sister was able to go to work but my Ma lived at the convent with the rest of her family. Before long she went to work in a hospital (live in) and could not wait for the week-end (or any time off) to visit her family in the convent. She married my Dad quite young and had her family (2 sisters & 1 brother) move in with her (not all at the same time). There were six children in her family just like there are six children in our own. I have always heard my mother calling out to God since as far back as I can remember. The one thing that has always struck me about my mother's situation is the lack of resentment my Ma has shown towards her parents.
She has always held them in high esteem.

This poem is for my Ma.

Deut. 5v16
Honour your Father and Mother as the Lord has commanded you. Then you will live for a long time, and things will go well for you in the land the Lord your God is giving you.

My Ma's Family (ma is middle right)

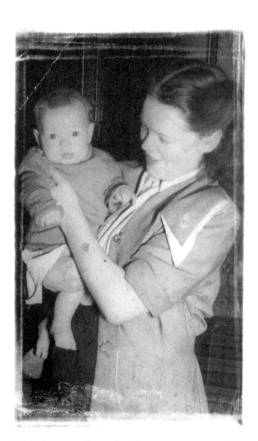

My Ma was allowed to be present at my first Mug Shot.

MA

Ahv'e goat a muther like emdy elses Ma
Ahv'e olso goat bruthers an sisters an a wee retired fae wurk Da
So wit makes mha Ma so speshal that a poem tae hur ah'd compose
It's the life she wiz forced tae live as a wee lassie, ah want tae expose

Five sisters an a baby bruther under fifteen they wer abandoned tae fate
Intae a convent tae be looked efter, exposed as fragile, fur them it wiz to late
Nae opshons or prospects, fae parents who widnay luv or ker
It wiz up tae the six o them wit life they wid lead, gon intae a wurld that wiznay fer

Scarred an skunerd in the tromma an brek up of her family line
Oot tae wurk she went, hopin against hope that ther wid be a sine
Maybe wan day everythin wid wurk oot an turn oot tae be aw rite
Hopin against hope aboot the turmoil, that wiz gein hur, hur biggest fite

Time went oan and things went slowly by
Susan, Sadie, Anne, Isabel and Pat intae life they went, their destiny tae try
Each wan hud the deposits of sorrow an pain, includin mha Ma
She met a wee guy in Meryhill wan nite, we noo call him oor Da

Efter me, five mer kid's wer born an overprotective she still iz
A motherly protectshon shinin through as she shoveles luv oan hur kid's
It's an odd coinsidence, hur hivin the same number o family that's in oor ain
Most o the time we gied hur joy an peace, but addin the wee odd bit o pain

Aye, we'v hid oor ups an doons jist like any other family ah know
Bit she stied at the helm wie love, observin as we moved to an fro
Av'e nae dout she hud the fear o loosin uz, the wie that she wiz lost
Only she kin understaun this, coz that wiz to her childhood cost

So how cum mha Ma hiz stuk it oot fur aw these decades o years
Putin aside hur ain life tae bring us up wae nae abandinment fears
It's az if aw hur ain experiences hiz stood uz in good sted
Gein uz a wee chance tae live an no bein emoshanaly ded

Noo she's a grate Granny wae a tribe o adorin weans
She cries wen we cry and shows joy at any sign of oor life gains
Bit mha Lord an hur Lord hiz a speshal place in Hiz hart
Fur a wee lassie brokin an abandoned, bit staunin up straite, gein hur family a start

Wie Insecurity an Guilt pushing against hur in life's path
She jist ploded on rejecting hur ain turmoil an emoshonal rath
She thinks ah don't understaun how hur hart wiz torn wie rejectshon
By a mother leavin a wee daughter with loneliness as a grievin infection

continued...

So ah apreshiate ye Ma, much mer than ye think
The trials ye'v endured alang wie the pain ye'v hud tae drink
Ahm jist glad ye didnay dae tae uz wit wiz dun tae yoo
That's wit makes ye speshal Ma, an we luv ye through an through

Yer faith hiz alway'z been rock stedy, solid, true an sure
Tae a saviour who wiz abandoned by hiz Faither, while He wiz Holy an Pure
So oor Lord understauns with troo empathy the feelins you'v hud in life
You'v passed His presence oan tae me, az ah wiz born, an yoo wur a young wife

Wance again, ah luv ye Ma an ahm glad o the things ye'v dun
If wit ye went though tae make ye a better Ma then it has benifitted everone
Yer reward is wae the Lord, as an wen ye meet
Nae prodistant or catholic church, wen intae heven ye'l get yer ain banquet seat

FAMILY

Having a big family is a good way to make sure there
will always be someone to answer the phone and
forget the message.

MOTHER

One mother can take care of ten children,
but ten children can't take care of one mother.

One of my friends who happens to be a Christian was taking up golf. I had been out for a round with him and he got the bug. He got a full set of clubs and said he needed a golf trolley. I not only agreed with him I also heard myself say I would buy him one. At the time I said this I could not afford it but thought the finance would turn up. It didn't, and I was left with egg on my conscience for saying something I was not able to do. So when I heard that he had managed to secure a buggy, I got him an umbrella and wrote the poem as an apology for opening my mouth to take my foot out.

Prov. 17v17
A friend always loves and a brother is born to share.

MY PAL JIM

Jim iz a **mate** thit a dearly **rate** a close pal an ah *frend*
Bit ah need tae say **sorry** Fur no buyin the **trolly** coz ah hud nae muney tae *spend*
The pedigree **went** with a broken promise **spent** an intenshons wer soggy an *wet*
Az a Chrishtian **man** he's no alowed anuther **plan** bit tae furgive me an *forget*

No bein **meek** bit wantin tae **re-seek** hiz aproval an hiz *favour*
Perhaps a cheeper wee **gift** tae gei him a **lift** or maybe a Gillette *shaver*
Naw it hiz tae huv a **meenin** wae a speshal **feelin** an item he realy wid *need*
Sumthin tae move him **deep** a wee bit deerer than **cheap** an keeps the rain aff hiz *heed*

Jist wan **thing** oan this hiz bag canny **hing** an it's no goat two plastic *weels*
So axsept this wee **umbrella** fae a promise free **fella** try it an see how it *feels*
So noo ah'v **confessed** an apolojised not in **jest** that's the honest *truth*
It'l teach me tae be **calm** an no act like a **bam** or at least tae shut mha big *mooth*

So ah'm jist **glad** even wae a lesson thit's **sad** as frends we ur still *conected*
Let's get the **trolley** up wae the **brolly** an geiz a swatch o the new clubs *selected*
The Wurld's **skool** seperates the wise from the **fool** so here's the lesson fur the *day*
No jist tae **spout** wae the wurds ah **shout** bit say wit ah mean an mean wit ah *say*

CHEAP TALK

Some people would say more if they talked less.

My family planned and executed a surprise 50th birthday party for me on Dec 99 in the Temple district of Glasgow. Being a well known "pie eater" in my youth, food was abundant (they knew that was the only way I would turn up).

As I have never been into parties, wedding receptions, or social functions that had alcohol it had to be a surprise because I would not have turned up. I would go to these functions but as soon as I felt the beverages taking effect I would take my leave and scarper. To me every thing seemed to be repetitious.

I can't remember having a birthday party before, so this one was a novelty. It was held in a local pub's lounge (The Siggy). After the initial surprise I tried to do a runner making the excuse that I had to get changed. I was persuaded to re-attend the function which I did. It turned out to be a good night out for one and all. A few of my Christian friends turned up amidst the throng of bears. This was a rhyme of thanks to those who came.

Church Tales

A young parish priest stood at his church doorway at St Ninnian's, a youth with spiked hair and dirty jeans ran up and threw a full bucket of bleach over the cleric soaking him to the skin. The parishioners were horrified at the act, but were delighted to hear that the youth was caught and charged with a Bleach of the Priest.

FRIENDSHIP

Friendship is like a bank account. You can't continue to draw on it without making deposits.

TA MUCH
(Tae the Bears)

Wit kin ah say aboot the uther day an the party ah'v jist hud
Auld mates fae Temple gates an no wan bottle o skud
Ah seen many a face thit mug shots embrace everywan wiz tidy indeed
Then ah looked aboot naybudy wiz givin a hoot perhaps we'r stull aff oor heed

Sum wur tryin tae walk an Bobby Lavery did tok wile dancin tae the twist
Davy didnay miss a trick wae hiz wallet thick bit skint he continued tae insist
At the bar mha wee Da stood in a grate mood shakin evry budies haun
He's a strait wee guy no a bit shy an he hud hiz best geer oan

Ah goat a call on the fone doon the hall fae the wan we call Miggy
Ah coodnay tell if he wiz wishin me well or just missing the Siggy
Wen we wur young we hud much fun we alwiz hud a rer time
Aye ther's been in's an oot's jist like oor soots bit az frends we ur fine

Aroon the table we wur able tae look fur an openin tae eat
Ah bloo mha disguiz becuaz o the pies an sumbudy goat aff wae mha seat
We hud pezza bits fae menu hits an pasta alang wae the tea
Savory rice with all things nice an enuff tae fill the 5th calvaree

Conversashons wur deep as oor afecshons did seep at oor luv fur wan another
A grate nite fur all the long the short an the tall coz everybudy wiz a bruther
Ah wiz full az a wulk ye coold tell wae mha bulk at aw the things ah ate
Gettin intae the car though no travelin far ah wiz wurried aboot mha stumiks fate

So thanks fur the wig the cumpany an the jig an kerds thit held the money
The patter wiz good alang wae the food even wen the jokes wurnay funny
Jacky Francie an Pat Billy Boaby Bosco an the Cat ye aw took mha attenshun
An if yer nondeploom hiznay bein gein eny room it's coz ther iz to meny tae menshun

So girls an guys withoot any disguize thanks fur yer luv an yer presence
Noo ahm putin up a poster tae catch the roaster who blagged mha bag full o presents
All things aside mha feelins a canny hide ye ur the best wee mob ah'v seen
Ah'l keep ye in mind in preyers thit ah find az ah praise an batter mha tambireen

Fondest Regards
Pat

fields of future dreams
the future is something which everyone
reaches at the rate of sixty minutes an hour,
whatever he does, whoever he is.
c.s.lewis

set course
i can't change the direction of the wind,
but i can adjust my sails always to
reach my destination
jinny dean

I have always felt that my life moved in phases (fields). I was game to try anything and no field had any fear for me. Up to the point when I was thirty three I had used up all the fields I knew about. If there had been any more, I certainly would have tried them.

My Lord and Saviour had a field with a narrow gate, but I could not go near it because of the ridicule I thought I would get from my friends. This field always had a fascination for me and when I finally entered it, I knew this was the place to be. It is a field that does not get churned up to become muddy, it cleans, comforts and consoles any one who enters. What I have found is that my life's mud, fades the longer I am in this field. Even though I chose the Lords field last, He accepted me as if I had chosen His field first.

Rev. 3v20
Look, I'm standing at the door and knocking. If anyone listens to my voice and opens the door, I'll come in and we will eat together.

SECURITY

A Christian went to buy a field one day. He asked the farmer if he could pay the price by instalments. The farmer asked if he was employed. The Christian answered "No."

"What about your wife and your three sons, are they working?" Again the Christian answered "No." "Ach" said the farmer "away with you, how can you afford to buy a field?"

So the Christian went to the next farm and asked the farmer if he could purchase a field from him. He asked for a pay up scheme like before. The farmer inquired if he was working to which the Christian replied with a "Yes" The farmer also asked about his wife and three sons. "Oh" said the Christian, " my wife and two of my sons work while my other son is at college."

The farmer was happy with this and informed the christian that he would send his solicitor to his home in the morning so that the documents could be signed.

The Christian went home and made the arrangements for the youngest of the sons to answer the solicitors call.

When he opened the door the next morning the youngest son was asked by a well dressed man with a brief case.

"Is your Dad in?" asked the caller.
"No, he's working." said the son
"Is your mum in then."
"No, she's working too."
"And what about your two brothers."
"It's not your lucky day." smiled the son "they are both out working as well."
"Well " said the man with the brief case, "It's not your lucky day either.
Tell your father and mother that the Social Security called."

fields of dreams

in the infancy of manhood and the world's promises lay ahead
i looked at each adventure as a pasture for dreams without dread
i gladly entered each field through a well oiled and shiny gate
not knowing earth's enticements were filled with danger from greed division and hate

i was contented to console my conscience with half-hearted intentions
while my being, demanded instant service for desires and lustful inventions
will you walk with me as i inform you about my fields of dreams
and as we separate the flesh from the spirit, you will see that life is not what it seems

to do this i need to ask my lord for revelation in this verse for to-day
allowing his agape love to unfold, as we look at his fatherly way
be assured, even if you have never met the saviour before
his desire is to awaken the spirit that lies dormant in man's human core

four lines to tell you about the field of violence and how it took it's course
respect, honour and equality were the goals but could only be obtained by force
as the ground churned up, division, rage, anger and gossip raised an ugly head
death was the master of this field, using it's minions, it desires to see people dead

moving from and on to the next field, the one labelled lust and next in line
thinking this was a place to be a man with women, fast cars and good wine
promiscuity is hand in hand with disease, as covetousness sears the sensitivity of the heart
lust can never be satisfied, waiting to rise again, and from love it keeps you apart

the field of greed, enticing rich pastures for self indulgence, finance and ambition
but it does not take long to be captured in an never ending circle without remission
"too expensive cries the buyer" and then goes and brags about his purchased deal
it becomes a way of life to say any thing to gain profit, no matter if you have to steal.

fluffy and rosy with colours and enticing music to match
the field of drugs waits patiently for any unsuspecting person to catch
"i use the drug, the drug doesn't use me" deception speaks as it implies you're in control
given time it will reach deep down and remove dignity, compassion and your soul

our personalities are made up from experiences and deeds of the past
if you are like me, you'll know there is something else, i had to move fast
when you roll about the mud and the churned up ground of the well trod fields
deposits of the garbage from every acre stick to you as life's walk reveals

there has never been a time i have not known about God and spiritual things
i enjoyed the conversations and debate that the religious subject always brings
from a baby i knew about his presence, his concern and his love
but when i met him i realised there was much more to this God from above

the head knowledge of a creator was clear and allowed me to move along just fine
confessions, penance, good deeds and prayers to the saints, that was the way to shine
so endeavours from my fields of dreams gave me the feeling that i was doing well
i was separated from the true God and living a life that was destined for hell

there always seemed to be a field far in the corner of my being
it had the narrowest of gates, and i couldn't go near, for the fear of someone seeing
a magnet pull would draw me towards an entrance i thought didn't need to be entered
but i ran out of fields with the mud stuck to my skin i needed to become God centred

i was accepted and allowed to enter, even thick with life's " glabber " and sin
standing in his space with head bowed low, i was given new life to begin
the decision took a long time, but it was a lot easier than it seems
to give up a mudy separation and to go into his field of dreams

it has got nothing to do with good works, it's a fathers grace that knows no bounds
i don't have the answer why he should love us so much, i just like the way it sounds
he cleans the mud from lives paths and from the fields of deceptions and deceit
all he has is a love eternal and with an abundance he want's to give when we meet

Going to my business after a good time of prayer and worship. One of my new employees, in the presence of the office staff commented on my grandsons (3) bad behaviour when he was in the office. It was like lighting the fuse paper to a rocket.

I was so angry that I gave her a dressing down and left her without any doubt as to where she stood.

I marched out of the office and spent an hour trying to gather my thoughts. Realising I had blown it I went back and apologised to the lady in question in full view of the office staff. This lady and I became very good friends. Even if we feel we are in the right, we can be wrong by our reaction.   Ecc. 7v9

Don't be quick to get angry, because anger is typical of fools.

CHURCH TALES

A young man giving a word from the Lord to the congregation,"As my servant Paul said in the book of Peter. Or was it James? I can't remember. Sayeth the Lord."

MIXED UP

An angry man opens his mouth and shuts his eyes. Cato

FRAJILE ANGER

Wer ur ye Lord wen ahm rantin an ravin
As ah react an no respond tae an incident no o mha makin
Tryin way aw mha mite tae stie oan Yoor corse
Bit its no easy fightin an resistin this ootside spiritul force

Even recognisin it, fur wit it iz an wit it wants tae dae
Listenin how it yooziz things in wit peepl say
Help me tae be steady Lord an no faw intae satans trap
Yoo ur the wie o life, the directshon ah want an need tae map

Paul tells uz that Yoo ur strong at the point wer we ur weak
Oh how ah need a revelashon o this, insted o a condemnashon reek
Sircumstanses kin moov in an change any buddys mood
Iz that no the time ah shood jump up an shout "Aw things wurk the gether fur mha good"

The bile o rejectshon bein stirred up by sum comment made
Ah thoat theze things wur behind me, bit ah gess ahm still afraid
Bein exposed az frajile isnay anybudies cup o' tee
Its bad enuff tae happen tae sumbudy els, an even wurs when it happens tae me

Ah tend tae faw fur it, espeshelly efter a good prer time
Hook line an sinker, doon ah go, at the point wen ahm feelin fine
Ahm so skunnerd to bein frajile at the point o loosin control
So Faither help me tae learn, coz Yoor the overseer o mha soul

There are so many new things on offer these days. At the time of writing this poem I was aware of the serious changes that were happening in to-days world. Morals and Ethics seem to be a thing of the past. Change, for better or worse, is steam rolling on in every walk of life. Up till to-day I do not see any brakes being applied to this runaway attitude. The only thing that seems to happen when public opinion is against it (e.g. genetic food and genetic engineering) is a postponed strategy that gives the changing bodies time to re-introduce their products at a later date. The change in modern man is governed by the Media more than in any other time before. Do you think this scripture is appropriate for today? After you read it, you can judge for yourself.

Paul writes nearly two thousand years ago in-:

2 Tim. 3v1-5

You must understand this: In the last days there will be violent periods of time. People will be selfish and love money. They will brag, be arrogant, and use abusive language. They will curse their parents, show no gratitude, have no respect for what is holy and lack normal affection for their families. They will refuse to make peace with anyone. They will be slanderous, lack self control, be brutal, and have no love for what is good. They will be traitors. They will be reckless and conceited. They will love pleasure rather than God. They will appear to have a Godly life, but they will not let its power change them. Stay away from such people.

SAD OR GLAD

If it weren't for the optimist,
the pessimist wouldn't know
how happy he isn't.

BUT

The man who says "I may be wrong, but..." does not believe there can be any such possibility.
Kin Hubbard

Streets Paved with Gold

Michael got a job in London and wrote home to his friend Pat in Dublin. "Pat," he wrote, "Get yourself over here. The work is plentiful. You just pick the money off the streets." So Pat packed his bags and arrived in London on a late Saturday night. Looking down he saw a twenty pound note at his feet. He went to pick it up, but stood up and walked away thinking to himself, "I'll just leave it and start on Monday."

RITE AN RANG

Hiv ye ever herd such things in yer life
Wen a man's no merried tae a wuman she kin claim tae be hiz wife
We'v also goat the guy's who want tae remember the Boyne
Couple it wae the bomber an ye hiv two sides o the wan coin
It's only tae themsel'z their cauzes seem fair an just
An tae gie thersel credability usin the name o God iz a must

Then there's the finominum called genetic engineerin
Were they kin grow o sorts o human things withoot it even breethin
Wit aboot the fertility experiment's that's supposed tae dae nae herm
When so called pioneers collect and experiment oan high counted sperm
Who'z kidden who wen they tell uz it's fur the benifit o mankind
Wen deep doon in ther hart's it's God's life plan they want tae find

An dont't forget the media, as if we ever could
The wild inacurate stories, dependin oan an editors mood
They churn oot gossip makin wee fibs thut ur so easy tae believe
Bit surely it's the finacial ploy that opperates tae deceive
They ur the wan's who tell uz they wer furst wae the news
But refuse tae retract wen they get it rang wi sumbudy elses views

Famin an the slotter o the innosents tuches even the coldest of harts
It put's things intae perspective, wer life ends and deth starts
Am wunnerin iz it jist me, or diz man know wit he'z dane
Actin aw wae it, az if he knows, whose tae be saved an whose tae be slain
Leaders bendin tae ootside preshures makin rules an regulations that don't soot
It diznay dae spiritual man any good becauze o it's earthly root

Kin we no understaun that this body iz only an ootside shell
It can only determine if we want tae go tae heavin or if we want tae go tae hell
Of course this ol flesh of oors want's everythin it can get
It's no conserned aboot oor spirit, in fact never wance hiv they met
Wan's gony die an wan's gony live, we ur in the final days
Dust returns tae the grun an the spirit goes back tae God, that's wit ma Faither says

So who say's right iz right an rang iz rang, Hiz anybudy goat an answer
Aw man diz is fight an argue, it's devision that causes the cancer
Ther's no even many countries goat ther act in place
Yet they awe hiv a government supposed tae be directin an protectin ther race

Naw, am afraid ther iz only wan wie tae go fur me
An the whole lot hinges oan the deth o a man as He hung alone tae a tree
He didnay hiv tae gei Hiz life, lashed mocked an scorned
An agonizin torturus deth, at a place wer few people morned
He say'z He's the wie the truth an the life, an this iz wit ah believe
Ye see wan day no so long ago ah met Him, an He's the Lord who cany deceive

I am always sensitive to see and hear that Christians feel condemned for feeling low. This early poem was aimed at, not only having a hard time, but also putting the hard times against the reality of the living Lord. At the expense of exposing myself, my spirit was having an argument with my head. (I am sure there is a medical term for this) when I wrote these words.

Even in the deapths treasures can be found.

DIG DEEP

Two Glasgow chancers went to a Yorkshire coal mine to see if they could get employment down the pits.

Geordie was asked at the interview, "And what kind of safety lamp did you use when you worked down the Sauchiehall pit?" Big Geordie thought hard and said, "Ach, Ah jist used mha gas lighter." Not getting the job Geordie said to Jimmy, "Watch wit ye say tae them aboot usin lites."

It was Jimmy's turn. "And what kind of safety lamp did you use down the Parkhead pit?" Jimmy was ready for that one. "Well sur," he said, "ah didnay need a safety lamp wen ah wiz doon the pit. Coz ah wiz oan constant day shift."

HOW CAN I BE SO LOW THIS DAY?

How cum ah'm so low this day?
Dain things rang an no the rite way
No jist paddlin, but swimmin in the depths o despair
When there's absolutly nay reason fur me tae be there

Ah tell mha soul tae rejoice, even tae respond
Fur ah'v goat a saviour an we huv a bond
Ye see He geid me a promise, when ah gave Him mha life
No so much tae protect me fae trubles bit tae keep me safe fae the strife

So how kin ah be worthy, wit wie kin a be troo?
Only through submitten, no jist tae Him, bit also tae yoo
Aye, it's easy tae walk wae Him haun in haun
Bit wen the rotatin problems arise, it's then we know wer we staun

He says "Aw things work the gether fur mha good" sometimes that's hard tae see
Bit if life hud nae hassles, then He widnay hiv hidtay huv died oan that tree
If only we could grasp how oor Faither treated His Son
It makes it easier tae accept that we grow on rocky and uneven grun

He understauns the things that take uz up an the things that take uz doon
That's the last promis He gied uz, He's no hingin aboot He's cumin back soon
Ye see it diznay matter how low we ur coz alone He canny lea us
He's goat the name above aw name's He's called the Lord Jesus

Turnin yer hart over tae the Saveyur kin only mean wan thing
Bein totaly selt oot, it brings peace an joy, an allowz yer hart tae sing
Who cares wit the others think, the scoffers, the lofty and the proud
Mha Lord didnay mutter a wurd wen forced up a hill wae the crowd?

It's so importint tae keep yer thoughts captive, talkin tae Him every day
No even the enemy kin brek in an distract ye fae that way
He giez us an abundance o life, He makes uz a new breed
Jist keep an eye oan the problems coz they don't start in the soul, they start in the heed

So how cum ahm so low this day wen aw these things ah know
Wen Hiz only desire is tae feed me right an watch mha spirit grow
Hiz luv fur uz iz permanent nae matter wit wei we look
An if it's hard fur ye tae believe me, then check the wurd, check the book

He allows the tests wae trials and cum what ever may
So we kin be refind an molded an chiped at every single day
He feeds me rite wae the things thit ur totaly esenshal
So wen ahm low mha faith gets a chance tea exersize it's full potenshal

It's only efter writin this, ah think ah see wer man's problem lies
He tends tae jump aboot wae blame, always pointin tae the skies
Kin we no see, the luv Faither hiz fur uz iz special, it's only wan o a kind
It's an Agape eternal luv aimed at oor soulz an no oor mind

It's hard fur me tae finnish this wee poem noo ah'm oan a run
Coz every time ah think wit God hiz dun fur me ah jist want tae praise hiz Son
So hopefully you'l lissen, an heed this wurd from a testemony that's troo
Fur He's the only wan tae huv died, fur the likes o me an yoo

SERENITY
Jesus did not promise his own that they would not suffer,
he promised a serenity beyond human reach because it has it's source in Him.

Leon Joseph

PEACE IS GOD
God cannot give us a happiness and peace apart from Himself,
because it is not there. There is no such thing.

C.S. Lewis

EVEN A BROKEN WATCH IS RIGHT TWICE A DAY

BROKEN BONES

I have had the pleasure of visiting the Spinal Unit, at the Southern General Hospital, Govan in Glasgow on a regular basis. I am in awe of the patients, men and women who have helped me get my priorities into perspective. Their bravery and perseverance is matched by a team of staff who give their undivided attention. The words below can't express what I feel. I hope it may express how they feel.

Broken body broken bones
Different people different tones
Pain to feel pain to hold
Need direction need to be told,

Fear strikes sharp, fear in my being
Effecting balance, effecting steering
Pills to stabilise, pills to sleep
Comfort from family, comfort to keep

Got to get up and move along
Got to be different, got to be strong
Want to stay focused, try a lot
For my partner, all that I've got

Sharpen reactions the ones not used
Refine perseverance when I'm not amused
Attitude change, attitude stern
So much to take in, so much to learn

Physio to-day physio to-morrow
Moods swing deep uncovering sorrow
Learn to sit up, learn to lie down
Transport essential, transport for town

Felt the stares, felt the looks
Can't watch the telly, can't read the books
Inching ahead as fast as I can
Going to stand like any man

Moving along aiming for an end
Lean on relatives, lean on a friend
Is there a God? Time will tell
Not like heaven more like hell

Physical recovery is almost nil
Same was said when he hung on the hill
Did he not rise from a dead struck state
Spiritually I pray for the same fate

No broken bones in His lifeless shell
Three days in the tomb three days to dwell
Then He rose by the spirit's splendour
I give Him my being, my being I surrender

Every heart has its own ache but there is nothing the body suffers that the soul may not profit by.

Dedicated to Alexander

here to-day gone to-morrow
told some jokes had some sorrow
lazed around walked a mile
got a number got a file

            was born without much say
            destined to walk man's way
            felt the perimeters keeping me in
            met cousins and rest of kin

                        had choices and picked a few
                        some stupid and some true
                        done the graft and had a rest
                        been to the north been to the west

put on a face many a time
made people think i was fine
charged and accused and done the same
took the rap took the blame

            lay in prison and been free
            was inquisitive and went to see
            learned from right learned from wrong
            wrote a poem wrote a song

                        groaned in frustration and anger too
                        took drugs with my motley crew
                        tasted rejection trying to please
                        tried to pray on hands and knees

felt a failure and been divorced
tingled when excitement was being sourced
laughed and laughed till i was sore
waited ages and ages to settle a score

            saw my kids and love them much
            got a ma with a mothers touch
            endeavoured to do what was right
            stayed calm and had a fight

                        something missing searched a lot
                        listened to theories and the odd plot
                        thought i knew all of life's way
                        what a shock with mistakes to pay

world promises offered much
swallowed in the lies and such
peace with happiness did not exist
different now i'm on fathers list

a vision came from god himself
work to be done not to shelve
was condemned now redeemed
life is different from what it seemed

destined to die so i can live
once i took now i give
someone cared to give his all
heard the voice got the call

now i say what i mean
testifying about things i've seen
love and joy and peace within
blood paying fee puts death to sin

void of fear of what's ahead
whether i'm alive or whether i'm dead
for every eye will look to heaven and see
that includes you and it includes me

"he (jesus) came to destroy
the works of the evil one"

SERIOUSLY FUNNY

My son-in-law got fed up with me preaching to him. He suggested to me more than once to "Lighten Up a Bit" and perhaps maybe even make him laugh. For someone who had not smiled since he had "hives" that was a tall order for me. This poem is filled with some comments and remarks made to me from family and friends (and strangers too) over the years.

Questions answered by a Glesga lad

What is ?	Answers
1. UB40	Burthday Kerd
2. Trifle	A three Barrelled shotgun
3. P45	Anuther Gun
4. A long lie in bed	Telling fibs oan a pillar
5. A reality check	A giro for using your inishitiv
6. A micro wave	Saying cheerio tae the wean

What is ?	Answers
7. A skein dhu	A pigeon dain a doonhill slalom
8. A cross dresser	An angry sideboard
9. A septic tank	A Cheeftan wae boils
10. A Synopsis	A female relative who went through surgery to have transgressions removed

SERIOUSLY FUNNY

How kin ye no rite sumthin that's funny an make me smile
How dae ye allway's want tae preach tae me an try an cramp mha style
It seem's as if it's the only thing ye ever want tae say
Always preachin and declerin how Jesus died oan Calvary way

Wit made Him so speshal thit makes ye so consistant
People did warn me that ye dae tend tae be oan the persistant
Ye might no want tae hear this, but sometimes ye day get rite up mha nose
Attemptin tae tell me how good He iz, an Hiz wies impose

So how aboot no bein so serious, an slakenin aff a bit
Av'e no been a bad guy, maybe a few drawz, a wee dram an the odd hit
Ah don't day enebudy eny rang, an ah even used tae go tae church
Noo ye tell me that's no enough, that mha life iz oan a lurch

Tell me then, wit aboot the other relijins, they aw say they'r rite
It's az if they want tae pull wan anuthers hers oot, an hiv a right good fight
Mullyins follow relijins, the Muslim's the Hindu's an the Jew
Lump that lot the gether, an ah say nane o them, includin yersel, hiv goat a cloo

Az for az ahm concearned, ahm wan o God's weans
Ah don't need relijon's name aroun me, so a kin get points fae Sunday games
Listen, av'e goat other pal's who think ther's nay God a taw
They say if ther wiz wan, how kin He jist staun back, an watch people faw

Bit sum things ye cum away wae diz make me wunner
Maybe yer rite, maybe yer rang, maybe ye ur jist a scunner
Aye, wee snippets dae cum through, an they often make me think
Iz this the wie tae brek the sircle fae a life gon doon the sink

continued...

Ah suppose ah need tae admit the change ah see in yer life

No jist in yer work or yer attitude, bit also the wie ye handle strife

The auld you seeps oot noo an again, then ye tend tae be sowir

It's wen ye faw ah notice ye tend tae gie it tae, as yoo say, God's livin power

Ah kin see that Jesus iz alive an livin well in yoo

An yoo say ah kin hiv the same thing, aw a need tae be iz troo

"Open up mha hart an let Him in" iz wan o yer speshal frazes

Somethin needs dun, coz mha life iz gon doon the tubes, it's jist gon tae blazes

Ye know it iz funny putin up aw these arguments an dowt

Wen deep doon in mha soul ah feel a stirrin, a spiritual clout

It's az if sumthin iz awakenin, an bein released fur the furst time

Aye, like a flowin, a freshness, a restart from a point wer ahm feelin fine

Ahv'e herd testamony aboot the Christ, an how He changes things

Ahv'e even seen an ex nut case greetin, haff wie through wen a Christian sings

Tell me, wit ur the things ah need tae dae tae let masel go

Fae a life that's destroyin me, an pushin me to an fro

Ah struggle against it wen deep doon within me ah know aw theez things ur rite

Bit dae ye hiv any idea aboot the turmoil within, man, it's like mha biggest fite

The last thing ah want iz a riddy or tae make a fool o masel

Then again ah don't want tae live a life o misery, an end up in hell

So ah gess it iznay funny tae make a desishon as serious az this

Wayin up the pro's an cons, scared o wit ah mite miss

Dae ye think it wid change mha life wan wie or the uther?

An if ah dae cum doon oan yoor side, wid that make Jesus mha brother?

I woke one morning with acute pains in my chest. As if that wasn't bad enough, I was also dealing with the cough that never clears your lungs. Just add a flu bug that would not budge and you will appreciate my full personal package. I did not know if I was alive or dead. I hope I have made that sound as bad as I possibly can because I am trying to milk any sympathy you are prepared to pass on.

In this state of being under the weather I got into thinking about my physical life and the spiritual release God had given me. This wee poem is the result of a self pity morning in bed. Hope you enjoy it.

Rom. 14v8-9
If we live, we honour the Lord, and if we die we honour the Lord, So whether we live or die, we belong to the Lord. For this reason Christ died and came back to life so that He would be the Lord of both the living and the dead.

MAKING SURE
All I desire for my own burial is not to be buried alive.
Lord Chesterfield

NO FEAR
No man should be afraid to die, who hath understood what it is to live.
Thomas Fuller

1Cor. 15vs55
Death is turned into victory!
Death where is your victory?
Death where is your sting?

LIFE TO LIFE

Before I was born, nothing I knew
Life's paths unfathomed or knowledge of man's debt due
I was not to know of the future trials, the tests and the snags
The day to day joys and burdens carried in the human memory bags

Injustices with poverty and strife, all still had to be learned
Agenda's never resolved because man in general is not concerned
I never knew about my ancestors rejection of the Creator's main aim
Nor the way God compromised, installing a blood sacrifice to reinstate salvation gain

So into life I went, picking up habits, direction and creed
Always feeling deep inside, that I had a soul and a spirit to feed
I listened to a few but followed the many, foolish and wise
Trying so hard to be accepted and have a character, that no one would despise

Picking and choosing the things that seemed right and fair
But never being contented because there was no spiritual care
Then it happened on that night, so still dark and cold
Jesus came and touched me, I knew His broken body for me He had sold

All the theories and philosophies, out the window they went
In that instant of time my spirit awoke, my outer shell spent
So what makes it so real on this path that I walk
Taking the hand of a living God and listening to Him when we talk

You know that you know by His presence and the plans that He makes
Its the way He fills you, confirming that His life was given for our sakes
Can't you sense the inner joy at being selected and chosen
It has nothing to do with men, as their words and deeds lie frozen

I've lived to the human rules and regulations, but that has all now changed
After the birth of my spirit, my life is being filled, rearranged
When He touched me, something happened deep down within my heart
The world can't understand when the spirit is given its brand new start

When I was born that surely wasn't the beginning
Being so small and vulnerable, I was a source of life for sinning
Sounds a bit harsh, but we have an enemy who's desire is to kill and destroy
Starting with a baby, innocent lives he wants to corrupt, it's his satanic ploy

So the years I wasted being engulfed in many physical and verbal regimes
All fall into insignificance like the rest of humanity's carnal schemes
The Father of Lights breathed His spirit into me at the point when life was allowed
Eternal it will return to Him after being refined from trials in the humanity cloud

On that day when my flesh and spirit part
With Father's grace and mercy, my eternal journey I'll start
All things will be made known as I fully embrace His love
Not man's reckoning or reasoning, but God's plan from above

Maxi Richards is a wonderful woman who loves our Lord dearly. She is a lady who lets her walk do the talk. Her walk has been with addicts, to whom she has opened her home as a "safe place" for over twelve years. I have had the pleasure to be in her company while doing odds and bobs on a voluntary basis at her home. There has been some most interesting youngsters to go through her care and protection. She sees her beloved addicts as young people being exploited, not only by the dealers but also by the authorities.

Her heart's desire is to see a drug free programme that will enable this young generation to get back to normality.

As an ex user myself I thought working with addicts would be a sinch. I must admit that some of the things they got up to put my faith on the line. Seeing Maxi plod on has been a great help and an understanding as to what Jesus said in:

Matt. 25v40
The King will answer them, "I can guarantee this truth; Whatever you did for one of my brothers or sisters, no matter how unimportant they seemed, you did for me."

Isa. 5v11
How horrible it will be for those who get up early to look for a drink

Name Change
In my younger days I played a lot of football. I was a "goalie" so when I became a Christian I was renamed "The Holy Goalie." A friend (his nick name is Briggs) who went to the same church was renamed, "Bishop Briggs" (a Glasgow Suburb). The best of all is Maxi Richards. One of her charges said she was the "Nun Without a Habit."

PRISONERS OF ADDICTION

I've heard and saw most of the aspects of addiction pain
The hopelessness and helplessness of a body and mind bordering on the insane
The deep seated rattle, with no ease nor peace of mind
Nothing seems comfortable and no words are kind

I've heard the lying and cheating and the shifting of blame
Always trying to stay on top, so that the habit may gain
Temptation lurks in every corner, even the crinkle of silver foil
One hit, or a drag into the lungs, it's square one, as the mind plans spoil

No one asked our children to participate in drugs Russian Roulette
With addiction in every chamber and no chance of escape, their time scale is set
It all seemed good and gave pleasure to kids who thought they were in control
Then the chains started to tighten and bite, crushing and digesting their human soul

So scared to awaken, yet they toss and turn and can't get to sleep
Daybreak appears, it's time to move, they have an appointment to keep
Where to turn to next, Heroin? Methadone? Finance says "It all depends"
While frustration and anger pour out from the hearts of family and friends

The habit controls and directs the paths that they take
Forgetting all the great purposes and intentions they make
We need to see they are genuinely sick, fragile, bruised and sore
Even their best endeavours usually ends up with someone trying to score

So how do we judge this generation, as to the dregs they are compared
Why not look deep into their anguish and see, they are just plain scared
As for me, I just want to be a pal in a real time of need
Hopefully showing God's love and allow Him to plant His eternal seed

METHADONE

20ml
15ml
10ml
5ml

Before I became a Christian I lived as normally as my upbringing allowed. Alas, on occasion violence was a topic that was evident in more ways than one. In chit-chat it manifested in story form, depicting tales of past victories and defeats. Hero worship or even respect for the "Hard Man", was part and parcel of the above conversations.

Violence itself was entered into, but never as much as talked about. Never once did I enjoy it, or benefit from it. It always left me feeling guilty and empty. On one occasion, I was charged with police assault against a police sergeant. When I went to court, He was sitting behind me. I turned to him and apologised for what I had done. This "sorry to the enemy," was against everything I grew up with, but repentance is what I felt even then. He was too taken aback to reply to me, but I went on to face my prison sentence with the peace that only being sorry can bring.

Ps. 11v5
The Lord tests righteous people but He hates wicked people and the ones who love violence.

Church Tales

Once committed to my fellowship I was in at the deep end. Anything on the go, I was in there. Our youth pastor asked me do drive a team of our youngsters to a rally in Cumbernauld. At the meeting (attended by five churches) our youth pastor asked if I would give a wee word at the end of the service on what I felt the Lord was saying. Sweat started to flow. This was my first real "Talking to people act" as a Christian. I prayed that the Lord would show me what He thought of this gathering. It wasn't till I stood up and opened my mouth, did I know what He wanted to express to His children.

In my minds eye I saw a large Corn on the Cob. Father impressed on me, and I said, that the cob was His church and that the coblets (Well, I did not know what they were called) on the cob were His fellowships joined to His church (body). I went on to say (during all the tittering) that we as churches belong not only to Him, but to one another. We are part of the same body. The word of unity was received with much laughter and I had a lovely peace at Father using me to express His heart.

As I started to mingle with the congregation I saw a very large and strait faced man making his way towards me. He weaved in and out of the crowd and when he stood next to me all I could think was "Eclipse."

"Kernel" he said. I put my hand out and said, "Pleased to meet you Kernel."

"No" he retorted. "Kernel is the name of the coblets. My name is Bill."

RUFTY TUFTY

Ah yoost tae hate conflict, wen things wer gon rang an realy runnin ruff
Insted o gettin oot, ahd flex ma mussels staun up strait, an try tae act tuff
If only ye cood hiv seen or felt wit wiz gon oan on ma inside
Ah jist wanted tae run away, go sumwere, curl up tae be safe, an hide
Bit that widnay dae fur a guy who professed tae hiven nae fear
Naw, ah faced up tae battles, wether ah wiz wearin auld sannies or even ma gallas gear
Sum o the disputes were verbal, bit ah took them aw tae hart
Only tae return them tae ther owners, wi violent wurds ah'd impart
Always oan a short fuse, reactshon, that wiz mha trait
Never listenin an respondin tae the other side, ah jist couldnay wait
Get the conflict over wie, an get it rite oot ma heed
Regurgitate vocal venom, it didnay matter who wiz fizically hurt or emoshonaly deed
So how did ah get oot o the prison that kept me bound up so tite
Allwiz wantin tae raect an no respond tae eny empendin fite
Ah gess ah need tae put it doon tae a mirical an proclaime wit iz troo
Ahm no sayin ah don't loose it, bit in general everythin iz moovin alang jist fine an ahm ticketyboo
Ye see withoot any introductshon ah met mha saviour wan cauld December morn
Luv wae Peace He introduced himsel wie a presence that wisnay forrin
Jesus came intae a soul that He wanted tae comfort, cleanse and convict
An ah knew by Hiz prezince, violence wiz amung the things He wanted tae evict
Ah hiv never fun oot wit made me behave in the wies that ah did
Maybe ma anger, maybe ma genes, maybe ah never grew up an jist stied a kid
Wit ah dae know is ah allwayz hated the conflict garbage, it wiz pure mince
Through Jesus ye could say am a new man, coz ah've always tried tae respond ever since

Tools of Bondage   Tools of Freedom

JIST A THOUGHT
Tools of violence can take you to hell. They can also take you to heaven.

Original Sin was the first sin I could understand when I was a child. It fascinated me so much that right through my life I always would offer up penances to God for my sins. If I was having a bad time, or lost something, instead of moping about or getting angry I would offer up my good behaviour as an offering for my sins. It was like a spiritual swap-shop. I would also pray to the Saints and ask them to help and perhaps talk up for me. I was using them as probation officers that were on my side. I would then pour prayers into the souls of Purgatory hoping that they would do the same for me when they were released from their predicament.

When I got the full revelation of Original Sin and how it is dealt with, according to the Bible, I was over the moon. Not only had I the full history of the fall but I had the answer to the restoration of man from sin. No penances were required only repentance was needed. It was going to have to be a perfect sacrifice (unblemished) to release man from his forefathers folly. Do you know all I have to do to enter this restoration? Repent and believe Jesus is the only antidote for sin. I hope the poem blesses you.

James 1v12-15
Blessed are those who endure when they are tested. When they pass the test, they will receive the crown of life that God has promised to those who love Him. When someone is tempted, he shouldn't say that God is tempting him. God can't be tempted by evil, and God doesn't tempt anyone. Everyone is tempted by his own desires as they lure him away and trap him. Then desire becomes pregnant and gives birth to sin. When sin grows up, it gives birth to death.

SHORT EXPECTATIONS

Two things that never live up to their advertising claims-: the circus and sin.

SIN (AT THE FAW)

Diz the wurd **sin** make ye want tae **bin** sumthin that means nuthin tae *yoo*
Izit an embarassin **feelin** thit sends ye **reelin** or maybe irelevently *untroo*
If ah telt ye it wiz a **destroyer** fae a satanic **employer** wid ye believe wit ahm *sayin*
So **eazy** even though yer gony feel **queezy** tae say the only wie rid o it iz throo *prayin*

Or dae ye think it diznay **mattur** even wae relijus **patter** az long az nae herm iz *dun*
Bit huv ye ever tied it **in** that it wiz man's **sin** thit cauzed the deth o God's only *Son*
Iz yer **defence** thinkin it's no an **offence** there'l be nay cosiquenses tae *face*
Geez a **minut** enuff time tae wash a **simmit** let's go back tae the faw o the human *race*

Ah'm quite sure yoo'l **know** az ye go to an **fro** the stories telt aboot Adam an *Eve*
An how the sleekit **snake** moved in tae **rake** the furst parents harts tae *deceive*
As darkness canny **fite** even the smallest **lite** they hid embarassed aboot ther *state*
Circumstances **changed** ther life wiz **rearanged** as they pondered ther chosen *fate*

Faither called **oot** "Adam ur ye **aboot**" as both o them tried tae hide naked *shame*
The rebelious **act** became a human **fact** az both attempted tae shift the *blame*
"It wiznay **me**" Adam called fae under a **tree** bit seperation hud entered *in*
Eve **refused** as she stood **accused** sayin "It wiz the snake thit made me *sin*"

Animal blud wiz **spilt** tae make a kind o **kilt** jist fur Adam an Eve's *sake*
This is the **point** a relashonship iz **joint** it's got tae be genuine an no *fake*
The blud **splattered** coz tae God man **mattered** shame wiz covered wae a *pelt*
Releesing a **flow** the final sacrifice **glow** as Jesus wae his Faithers hart did *melt*

So they cood **staun** hoddin Faither's holy **haun** fogiveness wiz in the *blud*
Covered by **skin** tae hide darkness **within** bit a new covenant wid wash like a *flud*
So efter choosing ther **way** they left wae pain an **dismay** even withoot eny *food*
Eden they coodnay get **back** by any earthly **track** coz angels wae flamin sords *stood*

Hard wiz the **grun** nae joy nae peace nae **fun** wae a life o labour tae *face*
Adam hiven tae **fix** the new lifestyle **mix** wae different priorities takin *place*
The day they **rejected** all ther seed wiz **infected** Adam's weans wid defend fur *thersel*
It's at that time we **face** satan hud a gatherin **place** wen he opened the gates o *hell*

The profesy rang **true** fur the likes o me an **you** sayin satins heed wid be *crushed*
Wit a **screemer** az Faither promised a **Redeemer** a covenant not tae be *hushed*
We wid get oot o **jail** withoot needin remishon or **bail** all debts paid an *cleared*
Jesus the lamb **sacrifice** wae nae **comprmise** coz tae Faither's will He wiz *geared*

Throo this wan **faw** the human became naked and **raw** and curses were set oan *man*
Hereditary they **say** iz a new name fur the **day** it's jist a genetic *plan*
Gein it a gallas **name** iz jist the **same** az sayin nuthin kin be *dun*
Sin kin be wiped **clean** cleaner than a washin **masheen** by acceptin the sacrifised *son*

Blud shed fur the auld man, blud shed fur the new
Gie me wan mer minut o yer time fur this wee story iz nearly throo

continued...

Mary wiz **pregnated** wae blud not **related** an antidote by the Holy ***Ghost***
So the deth Jesus **died** wiz **multiplied** and covers every human's ***innermost***
His **resurectshun** shows uz the **perfectshun** a ransom wae luv He did ***pour***
He wants tae **save** no jist the strong an the **brave** bit all thit open ther ***door***

Tae a **foe** wae nay wer tae **go** Adam capitulated every wan o oor God given ***rites***
Wae thorns in Hiz **heed** accept the **deed** coz satans dun nay mattur how hard he ***fights***
It's a bit like gon **back** oan tae the Eden **track** an walkin wae Faither every ***day***
Nae big holy **things** wae angelic **wings** coz ye accepted Jesus died the Calvary ***way***

17.5%
V.A.T.

Well here's tae **thought** coz its aw ah'v **got** ah hope ah'v gein ye things tae ***think***
It's no **heavy** like a burden or tax **levy** nor staunin withoot skates oan an ice ***rink***
Rejecting sins **path** an escaping the **wrath** wae Hiz antidote we put away oor ***pride***
It's basic an it's **neet** it's a faith thits goat **feet** an we definatly don't need tae ***hide***

The flesh wull **struggle** like a dug wae a **muzzle** it knows it's destined fur the ***grave***
We ur **united** by invitashon **invited** coz by Hiz blud He intends tae ***save***
So sin iz the **supressor** the wan an only **agressor** it fights an wants tae stie ***above***
It diznay know a **thing** aboot worship or songs we **sing** nor pure agape ***love***

If ye don't know oor **Lord** the only living **God** that's in a personal wie ah ***mean***
Then ye staun in the **faw** like up the creek withoot a **baw** fae demonic powers ***unseen***
But if ye **repent** wae wurds thit ur **ment** an put yer trust an faith in Him ***alone***
Revelation enters **in** like the remoovin o hard **skin** fae eyes thit wer hard az ***stone***

So here iz the **conclusion** withoot any **confusion** sin iz a killer wae wan main ***goal***
It's desire is tae **see** and watch wae **glee** az it attempts tae destroy yer ***soul***
It breks the commands o **ten** fur wumen an **men** an iz a partner in deths eternal ***fight***
The tree **supreem** thit every spirit hiz **seen** iz wer darkness canny be in God's precious ***light***

Real Sin
We are not punished for our sins, but by them.
Elbert Hubbard

FINANCIAL ADDICTION

Crawled fae a **stank** cumin oot the **bank** wei o it's decor an *glitz*
Promised **loans** makin uz finashal **clones** az proffits soar in spazmatic *fitz*
The frendly **face** iz part o ther **case** az long az the customer iz *snered*
Enythin **probmatic** becums **otomatic** az oan the cycle o fones we ur *shered*

Withoot **hostility** ye go intae an overdraft **fisility** an it aw looks prity *sound*
Be a penny **overdrawn** sounds az if yer dug hiz been **sawn** an yer hut fur thurty *pound*
Az long az yer no **funny** an yer account hiz sum **muney** then life iz jist *bliss*
Go intae the **red** even if yer sick in **bed** then the wee debt reminders don't *miss*

If thers a **mistake** like nae feet oan the **brake** then it's evrybudies folt an no ther *rap*
Letturs dae **flow** in a strait line like a **crow** az the problims they quickly want tae *pap*
It's such a **pity** az the staff ur so **witty** an plesant in all thit they say an *do*
Bit targits hiv tae be **met** like fuel fur a jump **jet** as money is ther god through an *through*

So aw great **offers** come fae loaded **coffers** lyin in a vault thit canny be *filt*
You an I **know** wether intae bank or shoap we **go** nae tears fur uz wull be *spilt*
The adverts oan the **telly** weigh hevy oan the **belly** az the visual an reality don't *meet*
Mamon iz the **boss** an hel no take a **loss** coz he'z the wan hoo sits at the tap *seat*

Ther wull be plenty of **percent** fur the lady an **gent** added an welded oan tae the *bill*
Aw sorts o **credit** fae a morgage tae direct **debit** engulf ye tae yer limit they *fill*
Muney's aw **right** az it helps in the poverty **fight** bit the problem iz beleevin it's *boss*
It grabs ye wae **fear** an yer conshins it kin **seer** if yer doon oan yer luck or ata *loss*

The bible **sayz** back in Jesus **dayz** thit it's the luv o cash thit causes the evil *fires*
Funny thing **iz** takin away the finanshal **biz** it's really doon tae oor ain *desires*
Diz the **sorrow** cum fae being tot tae **borrow** by a finashal power of *addicshion*
We ur no **content** in what wiz **meant** wen He released uz by the *crusifixshon*

Maybe we kin **see** thit nuthins fur **free** an evry single thing cums it a *cost*
That's how He **died** showin sin **magnified** wae open erms He gathered in the *lost*
He'z mha **banker** ah couldnay be **franker** az a submit all my harts *content*
Nay interest tae **giv** or pockets tae **siv** ahm in one hunner *percent*

Oh **aye** let me **justify** wan o the abuv statements ahv jist *made*
Ther iz sumthin **free** an it wiz confirmed oan a **tree** an this iz the wurds He *sade*
"It is **finished**" meaning satan has **deminished** we are free from addiction *traps*
We can now **chooz** win draw or **looz** on the feedom path He *maps*

SUCCESS
Success has nothing to do with what you gain in life or accomplish for yourself,
it is what you do for others.
—Danny Thomas

A bad habit I have is interrupting. I try so hard to get it right and have even become expert at butting-in without exposing my bad manners too much. I can only say that I am aware of it and I am trying to perfect the art of listening. I always feel that I will "forget" what I am thinking about by the time the conversation is finished. So to all of you that I have interrupted in the past "I'm Sorry".

James 1v19
Remember this my dear brothers and sisters; everyone should be quick to listen, slow to speak, and should not get angry easily.

FIRST TO LISTEN IS A WINNER

LUGS OF THE CENTURY
A pair of good ears will drain a hundred tongues.

Church Tales

GALE IN THE NIGHT

Visiting a neighbouring church to show the hand of friendship a young Christian commented to the steward that the lady practising a song in the main hall sounded more like a "Gale in the night" rather than a "Nightingale".

To his embarrassment the steward said "That gale in the night is my wife". The young Christian tried so hard to wriggle out of his embarrassment by saying "It's not really her singing, it's more the lyrics and music of the song".

The steward politely opened the door to the hall letting the young Christian enter and said "It was me who wrote and composed the song."

SLOW TO LISTEN

Ahm so slow tae hear an so quick tae talk
Ah get things roun about in the wie that ah walk
Ah didnay even know how hard it wiz tae be a Chrischin
Or maybe wen ah wiz spoken tae a jist wiznay listenin

Ah wiz so high at meetin mha Glorious Lord
Ah jist goat up an started tae run weeldin the two edged sord
Communicashon that's the wurd ah wiz tae remember
Bit wiz that last August October or Novenber

Runnin ahead seemed tae be a lot easier than jist plain walkin
Thinkin wit tae say while uther people wur talking
As ye kin see ahv'e goat an answer rite up tae the time ye hiv sighed
An then wae mha thots ahl tok coz ah'v never been tung tied

Bit in mha inthusyism tae pleeze serve an tae bless
by no listenin, it sumtimes leiz me tied up in a wee verbal mess
Knowin wit ah mean in the things that ah say
Often disnay cum oot in an understaunin way

Sometimes ah dae hear an sometimes ah even dae well
Bit if you ur anythin like me it's usually tae soot masel
This Faither of oors who formed all of creashon rite doon tae the season
Placed me wer ah um to-day an it wiz fur a spesific reason

It's wae this in mind ah hed on towards the goal
Gettin mha priorities sorted oot while the Lord wurks oan mha soul
He knows aw mha weaknesses an He knows wer ah staun
That's the reason He let's me rush in, coz He's goat a haud o mha haun

It's usually in mha failins the Holy Spirit an I meet
That's the Faither's wie o dain things tae make me complete
Waitin an directin patiently while in the wurld ah bound along
Testin an streatchin mha faith at the same time in mha hart He places a song

So ah must admit "NO LISTENIN" iz a thorn in mha side
Coz ahv'e goat a voice that persists an modisty canny hide
Bit covered in Hiz protectshon usin Jesus as mha shield
Mha grate Faither huz plans fur me at the point wer ah yield

Ah suppose it's time tae be quiet an draw up a new bead
Allowin the Holy Spirit to move an minister wae the things goin oan in mha heed
Oustin oot the rubbish an burnin up the dross
Leavin mha mind totaly free tae listen. Surely that's nae loss

uphill

uphill, uphill, uphill all the way
or live in the pit where the flesh want's to stay
does not the marathon runner go through a barrier of pain
reaching for his goal and a medal to claim

being saved released and lifted to my feet
this spirit father has given me doesn't recognise defeat
o yes i might stagger through i might complain moan and mumble
but my entry fee was paid for by a god who does not stumble

i don't need to keep up a pace that is taxing and fast
what i do know is that the steps i take are all away from the past
so if i do fall get tripped up and even end up bruised
my mind is steadfast it's on the race i don't get confused

at the same time in another lane there is a race that seems to be faster
the gathering of mankind rushing ahead it's destination is disaster
thinking along godless lines it runs towards the brink
accepting what the world says a satanic strategy they drink

believing in a human trainer consensus when there is none
not seeing the starter of mankind when father to man he gave his son
eating sleeping dieting or drink they leave their fate not concerned about excesses
hoping against all hope that man will become good or at least return to his senses

as this life takes me on and through my paces
the training trials with hurdles and tasks with different faces
there is the race that's narrow and the race that's wide
it all depends on what you want to do and what's inside

as for me i've tried them both and each seemed hard to run
the wide one looked easier with the wine music and fun
but the narrow one is right and totally worth while
it has an aim a goal a direction and a resting place with style

it's all very tempting to receive my rewards to-day
seeking men's praises with deeds i do and things that i say
but the treasure i desire lies in fathers perfect face
when he turns and say's to me "well done my son, you've ran your earthly race"

a successful road
all roads to success are uphill.
– John Masson

I WISH YOU JOY

I DO NOT WISH YOU JOY WITHOUT A SORROW
NOR ENDLESS DAYS WITHOUT THE HEALING DARK
NOR BRILLIANT SUN WITHOUT THE RESTFUL SHADOW
NOR TIDES THAT NEVER TURN AGAINST YOUR BARQUE
I WISH YOU FAITH AND STRENGTH AND WISDOM AND LOVE
GOODS GOLD ENOUGH TO HELP LIFE'S NEEDY ONES
I WISH YOU SONG BUT ALSO BLESSED SILENCE
AND GOD'S SWEET PEACE WHEN EVERY DAY IS DONE

A POEM CARVED OUT ON THE WALL OF AN 18TH CENTURY BALTIMORE CHURCH.

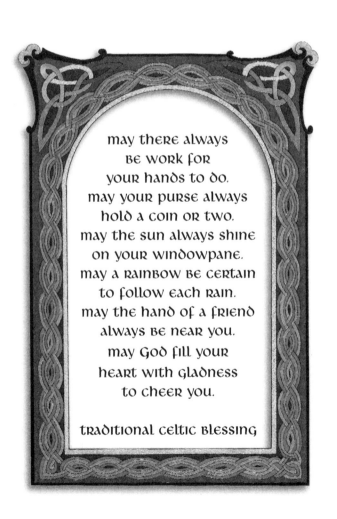

may there always
be work for
your hands to do.
may your purse always
hold a coin or two.
may the sun always shine
on your windowpane.
may a rainbow be certain
to follow each rain.
may the hand of a friend
always be near you.
may God fill your
heart with gladness
to cheer you.

traditional celtic blessing

FORCEFULL WARRIOR (THIS IS THE TIME)

Matt. 11v11-12
I can guarantee this truth: Of all the people ever born,
no one is greater than John the Baptiser. Yet, the least important
person in the kingdom of heaven is greater than John. From the time
of John the Baptiser until now, the kingdom of heaven has been
*forcefully (KJ-Violently) advancing, and *forcefull (KJ-Violent)*
people have been seizing it.

During a quiet time I was reading the above passage and remembered I had heard a pastor preaching from this text just after I got saved. Because of my past and the revelation of finding an amazing God who loved me it went over my head. Now when I read it again I realise it say's that the Kingdom advances "Violently" and "Violent men take hold of it." The word "Violence" is not a buzz word for to-day neither is it politically correct. On the other hand "Peace" is the word to be proclaimed and professed, even when there is none.

His Love is the strongest force ever to be released in the universe. It comes to them who seek it. It is available to the least of us who think and know we deserve nothing. Is it not wonderful to be Loved by the Living God? So let us about turn (repent) and march with and in the most awesome and powerful force ever. Are you the least in the kingdom? Well you should be at the front so lets go and use His Love *forcefully. Don't forget, as Christians we do all things in Love, especially being forceful.

Joel 3vs10
Weaklings should say they are warriors

Eph 6vs12
This is not a wrestling match against a human opponent.
We are wrestling with rulers, authorities, the powers who
govern this world of darkness, and spiritual forces that
control evil in the heavenly world.

Vine-: *force: 1. HARPAZO, to snatch away, carry off by force, is used in the next sentence in Matt. 11v12, to that referred to under No1, "men of violence (A.V. "the violent") take it by force," the meaning being, as determined by the preceding clause, that those who are possessed of eagerness and zeal, instead of yielding to the opposition of religious foes such as the Scribes and Pharisees, press their way into the Kingdom, so as to possess themselves of it. It is elsewhere similarly rendered in John 16v15 of those who attempted to seize the Lord and in Acts 23v10 of the chief captain's command to the soldiers to rescue Paul.

FORCEFULL WARRIOR (THIS IS THE TIME)

Mat 11v11-12

```
      A                           D            A
Gracefull and forceful warrior and least of men
E                                              D
You are expected with Love and Commands of Ten
    A                           Em     A
To go collect and gather in lost souls
                                  D      A
As the kingdom advances forcefully to it's goals
```

CHORUS

```
    G                         D          G
This is the time for His love mercy and grace
                                 C       G
This is the time to see the Saviour's face
                                  D      G
This is the time when forceful men push ahead
                                C       G
This is the time to proclaim real life for the dead
```

```
  A                              D          A
Hear the trumpet call to the world's broken n' sick
  E                                          D
Hear the widow and orphan from scraps they pick
  A                              Em     A
Hear injustice and poverty from mankind plans
                                  D      A
Hear our Fathers call to the world He scans
```

(CHORUS)

```
    A                          D       A
Holy Power and angels stand at your side
  E                                     D
Giving God the glory that darkness can't hide
  A                            Em    A
Creation's expectation's for you to be known
                                D    A
Confirming Salvation seeds He has sown
```

Ecc. 3v1
Everything has it's own time,
and there is a specific time for every activity under heaven.

PAULINE'S POEM

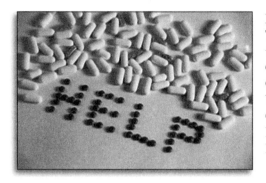

I am trying to justify the reason for my actions
The guilt is so over-powering as I begin to understand why and how
though I'm dealing with it in tiny fractions
Oh to be guided and fully understood
Cos the intoxicated days are never overlooked
Will the shame ever go away?
Or will it eat away at me from day to day?
I need to get my life back on track
Please help me don't turn your back

A young woman trapped and abused by addiction puts a few lines of her emotions on paper 31/01/01

MAD AS A BRUSH

The hair on hur **hed** iz a brite **red** an she's az slim az any *brush*
She stauns tae the **side** wea nae wer tae **hide** until ah make the *rush*
She's no so **stable** goin under the **table** bit in mha hauns she's *awrite*
It's like a wee **dance** wae a skip an a **prance** bit we never go oot at *nite*

Water an **coke** diz make hur **choke** so liquids tend tae be a *warning*
Cauld **friez** an minse **piez** ur things she hates furst thing in the *morning*
If yur **single** an dont tent tae **mingle** an ye think carpets ur a *bore*
Then get yersel wan o **theez** coz they save the **neez** an nothin is a *chore*

Big long **sweeps** mha fler clean she **keeps** redy fur any domestic *tests*
Ah put hur **away** fur the rest o the **day** an intae a corner she *rests*
Aff hur **Ma** thats the partner of hur **Da** Meshel gave it tae *me*
Nae mer **Oose** loos aboot the **hoose** fae dust ahm completely *free*

A dear friend got me a gift (she received from her mum) that blessed me through and through. As I only have ceramic tiles on my floors at home, sweeping becomes a time consuming and nerve building adventure as I chase the "Oos aboot the hoos." I am now an owner of one of those large red mop type brush things (above) that collects the dust rather than seeing the dust jump over the brush. It even swivels in any direction I want without lifting the head off the floor. I was so excited about it that I gave it it's own poem.

When I became a Christian I felt that problems would just be a mere blip in my life. Now that I was in the light I could cope with anything that came along. The reality was different. I must say that in those early days I could not understand why small problems seemed to erupt engulfing my new freedom.

I found that in some circumstances I was defenceless and vulnerable. I now know that circumstances challenge faith at every opportunity. There is no short cut I can find in the Bible that informs me of an "instant problem wipe out" in lifes walk.

Comfort comes in the face of trials. God's word says -: **"I will never leave you or forsake you"** along with, **"Consider it pure joy when you go through trials"** and my favourite **"All things work together for good. "**

So when persistent trials arise I genuinely sometimes have no option but to stand and ask my Father "How are You going to get out of this one Lord?"

I now know that His defensive force is a force that does not defend but attacks. It not only repels but pushes back the opposition to my spirit. When I have done all that I can, I STAND and turn things over to Him. I stand on His Word, I stand on His Power, I stand on His authority and I stand on His Love.

So even if your flesh doesn't feel it, it will catch on as you stand in awe watching your Father clear the debris. After all the battle belongs to Him.

Eph. 6v11-14
Put on the armour that God supplies. In this way you can take a stand against the devils strategies. This is not a wrestling match against a human opponent. We are wrestling with rulers, authorities, the powers who govern this world. For this reason, take up the armour that God supplies. Then you will be able to take a stand during these evil days. Once you have overcome all obstacles, you will be able to stand your ground.

WHO IS IN CHARGE

Most Sunday mornings when I lie in bed, the old flesh informs me that I have had a hard week. "Forget about getting up and enjoy a good day of rest" comes the relaxing thought. I entertain the idea cultivating it into what I could do with the morning instead of going to church. When decision time comes, the flesh does not stand a chance. I say to myself "Well body, you can lie there on the bed but I am going to worship the Lord." Do you know that never once has my body not joined me. It always seems to be with me when I enter the assembly to praise His name.

STAND

"It's chains and bondage" are the things they say
That tie a man up and make him feel this way
Nothing fits depression reigns
How on earth am I going to break loose from these chains

I try this and that struggling against the cords so tight
But condemnation is activated it knows I'm in a fight
Coupled with temptation the duo move in
Their total goal is to see me fall, overcome sin

The sins of my youth the things of the past
Brings a taste that only regurgitation can cast
The stench of these ingredients shows me I'm not a one man band
At this time in my life there is nothing I can do except use His word
and stand

All things He does all things He knows
Cutting me free from my enemies and defeating my foes
Pushing the forces to the left and to the right
This is not a physical war it's a spiritual fight

There can only be one winner and that's been declared
From Calvary He shouted "TETALESTI" a victory inferred
So no matter how I struggle by things I can't see
The Holy Spirit placed in my life give me His guarantee

If there are a few things to sort out in this new life release
Then all His promises count as He wraps them in everlasting peace
So when I'm down I know it's not what the Lord planned
He gives me a safety-net that comes into force at the point when I stand

No way my Saviour is robbed of His glory I can't be snatched from His grasp
By the darkness of a spent force who uses the debris from the past
Father grants me grace to receive the free gifts from His hand
No more condemnation now because I know were I STAND

I PRAISE YOUR NAME

This was just a song I wrote in testimony to our Saviour. It was one of those day's that everything seems right and praising God flows from the heart.

*Psalm 118v17
I will not die, but I will live and tell what the Lord has done.

BY GEORGE!

At the time I was saved there was a mini revival in the area. About forty people came to know the Lord in a short period of time. We came from all walks of life. One night as we sat in an ex drug dealer's house going through the Bible, somebody suggested we should pray. So here we were, in the middle of a room that only weeks prior was being used to sort out drug packages for sale, praying to the living God. One of the group was so filled with the Holy Spirit he shouted out in prayer (trying to say "Jesus" and "Lord" at the same time) "BLESS YOU GEORGE." I will leave your imagination to think about what happened next. I would like to say that it is a joy (and that can include laughing) when the Holy Spirit moves.

I PRAISE YOUR NAME

Am   G
I want to say how much You mean to me
Am   G
Praising your ways while You set me free
Am   G
I know your presence with me all the time
Am   G
Even though I fall I find Your hand in mine

CHORUS

Am   E
I praise Your name I praise Your name
Am   G   Am
I praise Your name above all names   (x2)

Am   G
With these words I declare an open heart
Am   G
Burn up the dross that keeps us so apart
Am   G
Jesus I kneel for the world to look and see
Am   G
Exchanging death for new life from the tree

CHORUS

Am   G
I shall not die but live to tell Your deeds
Am   G
Testifying to men and sowing gospel seeds
Am   G
Draw me in closer as Your arms open wide
Am   G
Like the prodigal son I may stand at your side

LISTEN

Listen to me Lord as I reveal my pain
Listen to me Lord as I seek Your peace as gain
Listen to me Lord I'm so grieved and weary
Listen to me Lord for You are reality and not theory

Hear me Lord when I cry from my heart
Hear me Lord when circumstances keep us apart
Hear me Lord when I've no where to turn
Hear me Lord when from you I seem to run

Help me Lord to receive Your promises and desires
Help me Lord to dampen my insecurity fires
Help me Lord to live on Your word alone
Help me Lord to be real and not a conformed clone

Will You answer me Lord my heart sinks low and is heavy
Will You answer me Lord I'm standing but not so steady
Will You answer me Lord patience has now run it's course
Will You answer me Lord release Your Holy Spirit force

I know You Lord and the truth that You speak
I know You Lord when your assurance I seek
I know You Lord You always come through
I know You Lord Your presence is pure and true

I'll listen Lord as I go on my way
I'll listen Lord to the things You do and say
I'll listen Lord through all the noise and din
I'll listen Lord as one by one, my anxieties You bin

I remember when millions of pounds in grants were awarded to the district of Drumchapel, Glasgow for the benefit of the local population. In church we prayed it would be used wisely but felt that it would be swallowed up by red tape machinery.

Then a new industrial estate was to be built next to the local shopping centre and again I felt that the local facilities and shops were overlooked. At that time we were moving our business to another part of Glasgow. We were approached by a local politician to keep the factory in the Drumchapel catchment area. Our business was offered grants and a building to rent if we stayed in Drumchapel. After accepting the proposal, the grant was refused. This was after they had allocated £10,000 for new furniture for themselves and we had to agree to a secured loan instead. Through this experience Drumchapel Initiative lost the opportunity to secure the investment by the group who took our company over. We were asked by the new owners if we would recommend that a new factory should be built in the area. Unfortunately we had to recommend that a new site be found, as the local politician had led us astray with unfulfilled promises. I do not know how much influence our report was, but a new two million pounds factory was built in Kilmarnock in preference to Drumchapel.

I then purchased a large house in Tighnabruaich with the intention of making it a respite centre. I went to sell the property on to a Christian Charity (which deals with drug rehabilitation). It took three years to complete the deal. This delay was caused by red tape and the incompetence of so called professionals.

I would often get frustrated and blame as many officials as I could. Bitterness seemed to be getting into my heart, so I share the blame, as I covered them with more criticism than I did with prayer.

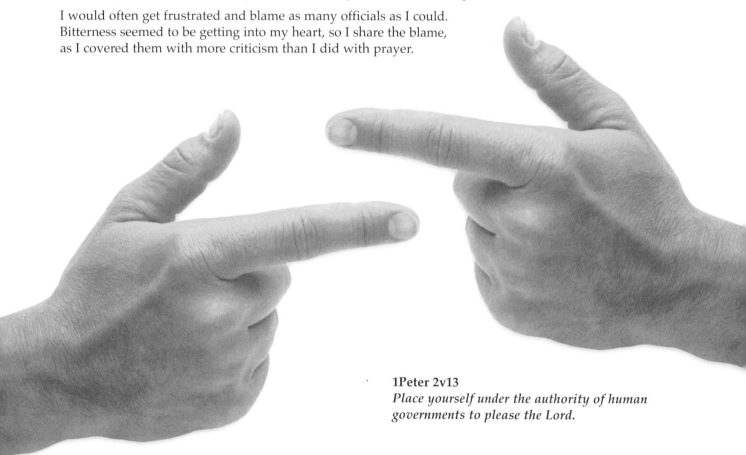

1Peter 2v13
Place yourself under the authority of human governments to please the Lord.

I should have prayed for them more than I moaned. For He is the One who ordained them to lead. Hope you like the poem.

POLITICAL BARK

Never retract, never explain, never apologise, get the thing done and let them howl. Nellie McClung

HOOZ TAE BLAME?

Im ah **thick** ur jist plane **sick** wen ah try tae beg an *borrow*
Fae **MP's** an offishal **deputees** thit canny see peeples *sorrow*
Custodians **elect** wen they pick'n **select** haudin aw the public purse *strings*
Wit diz it **say** wae wit they **dae** stickin it aw intae the most stupid *things*

Over **joyed** fur the **unemployed** az coffurs filled fur Drumchapels despair an *pain*
It ended wae big oafis **jobs** fur ootside **nobs** an ten grand tae furniture, fur the *vane*
So wit othority dae ah **hiv** wae the verbal ah **giv** aboot people we put in *charge*
The Inishitive's **faw** an the Centre's **claw** ending wi oor wee company gon *large*

The Drums shopin **Centre** no thought did **enter** as plans wer made fur a Park's *Retail*
B&Q fur the likes o me an **yoo** bit fur the locals ther councilors wance again did *fail*
Residents tae **shop** hiv tae bus **hop** fur clayz an ther messages they *hunt*
Because wee **leaders** wer lookin fur **feeders** gettin a political posishon up *frunt*

It wiz time tae **moov** ootay the Inititive **groove** gone tae a Merryhull *factory*
Oor bizness wiz **well** as it started tae **swell** we wur summund by the Labour *Party*
"We canny let ye **leev**" wiz it a trick up ther **sleev** they promised muney fur *assistance*
Wance we **agreed** they seemed **releeved** the grant became a loan becauz of *resistance*

Wit coold we **say** wit they dun that **day** leein us wae thoot a leg tae *staun*
We hud said **yes** they coudnay ker **less** wae nae opshons we goat the new factory *gon*
Furbuy aw the **exsess** we made a **sucsess** an ootside bid for the bizness wiz *agreed*
We moved **away** az we couldnay **stay** fae Drumchapel politishons we wur *freed*

Noo ahv'e goat a big **hoos** wie nae cash **loose** ahm lookin fur help tae help *uthers*
Wance **again** ah see the **strain** hiven tae approach and beg the purse string *scunners*
Naybudy **kers** aboot drug rehabilitashon **affers** it's like tryin tay find a ducks *tooth*
If it's no methadone **frendly** yer scheme iznay **trendy** an that's the honest *truth*

Power that's the **tower** it giez them a platform tae converse and *say*
"We'll get it **rite** wae political **fite** jist vote fur uz the *day*"
Wance they ur **in** ther's nay moral **sin** they jist go ther ain *root*
Quellin public **feers** wae statistic **geers** they don't ker nor give a *hoot*

I'm ah oot o **order** gon over the **border** bein angry wae leeders who don't *ker*
They collect **credit** fur personal **merrit** an glory they ur alwayz lookin fur *mer*
Sanctimonius **behaviour** fae a tin pot **saviour** mha stumuck's up side *doon*
Ther **minipulashon** iz like a **stipulashon** sayin "aw wull be fixed an made good *soon*"

Ah widnay **mind** if they cood **find** or lissen tae sumbudy who new the *score*
An addict will **convict** an open conshons **quick**, fur freedom hiz life he wants tae *pore*
Wance he kin **decide** ther's nay wer tae **hide** he wants tae cum aff the *kit*
Aw thit kin be **dun** fur sum muthers **son** is a waitin list or the killer methadone *hit*

continued...

In **deelins** ahv'e hud aw kind o **feelins** wae the othorities who ur supposed tae *no*
Govermint **indeed** ur people wae nae **speed** they don't hiv the will tae get up an *go*
Sum hiv **laffed** an sum hiv **chaffed** while most jist sit politely sterin wae a *goad*
They don't **understaun** aboot the lives in **haun** coz they don't know " wer the rubber meets the *road*"

Bit ah ber the **blame** an ah share the **shame** fur fallin well short o God's *wurd*
Aye ahv'e been **critical** o the **political** an it mite sound a wee bit *absurd*
Coz wit ah don't **dae** is sit doon an **pray** aboot oor leaders who ur chosin tae *lead*
Insteed o moanin an **groanin** it's time ah wiz **showin** preyers fur them that *intercede*

Ah lee em **alane** tae play ther **game** furgettin they ur open tae prinsipalitees an *powers*
They need **cover** as they **discover** ther's life apart fae debate an politicle *towers*
A holy **edict** fur oor Lord tae **convict** aw uz Christians who sit wi branes thit ur *frozen*
Tae rise wae **preyer** an show we dae **ker** fur oor leaders hoo God hiz *chosen*

So if ahm **serious** aboot adicts **delerious** attemptin tae struggle fur ther *plite*
It's doon oan mha **nee** if they hiv tae be **free** fae de`tox pain an addicshon *fite*
This war'z no fae **guy'z** wae red tape **disgize** it's a struggle of satanic *proporshons*
Wantin tae **kill** wae a drug **thrill** expressed in deth set *contorshons*

Tae the Lord ah **bow** wae preyers oan **tow** fur oor electid trustees *protecshon*
Furget aboot mha **gripe** wae the intensity **hipe** nae mer instint *disectshon*
Aye ah kin **complane** aboot the proud an the **vane** that's only wen ahm in *rank*
Cumishond tae **reveel** a God hoo iz **reel** bit chekin mha eye iz no filled wae a *plank*

HARD TO CHANGE
I know that most men can seldom accept even the most obvious truth, if it would oblige them to admit
the falsity of conclusions which they proudly taught to others, and which they have woven,
thread by thread, into the fabric of their lives.

Leo Tolstoy 1828`1910

POP BANDS

Before I became a Christian I remember John Lennon saying that "The Beetles were more popular than Jesus." Then we had Jim Morrison from the "Doors" shouting out to his audience at his last concert; "Cancel my subscription to the resurrection."

These are just two of the young men who said what they felt, at the time they felt it. John Lennon was involved with the Mystics in India and Jim Morrison was heavily under the influence of narcotics. Both obviously didn't know Jesus at the time but to the generation who heard their comments and knew of their attitudes it would have some type of anti Christ effect.

FILMS

From "The Life of Christ" to the film "Dogma" we have been subjected to a continuous flow of blasphemy from one of the largest mediums in the world. George Harrison financed "The Life of Brian". Who "on earth" would want to do such a thing?

RADIO & MUSIC

In my eyes I feel as if it has been a continual mocking of the living God in an attempt to un-deify Him. To-day the music scene continues on this same theme. Look at the opposition Cliff Richard had when national radio stations would not play the Lords Prayer. Even Talk Radio throws in the name of Jesus Christ from atheist broadcasters. Mediums are conjuring up guide spirits for entertainment on these same programmes.

CULTS

Just look at four of the major cults (among many) that have sprung up over the last century. J.Ws, Mormons, Christian Science and the Moonies all add their own interpretation of the Bible. Common denominators are they all claim to have "personal" insight to what God meant in the Bible they do this by adding their own books of interpretation. They also deny that Jesus Christ is God.*

CHURCH

Small but sometimes influential statements seep out of the Church in seasonal regularity. Thank God they are few and far between. Statements regarding the "Virgin birth" and the "Ressurection", etc are the topics that liquidate Fathers power and position as the All Eternal God. Their human theology under the name of Christianity takes the full potency out of the crucifixion which in essence nullifies the Holy Spirits power.

When I hear of their endorsement and the coming together of outside faith's and religions I cringe. Surely if the unity of foreign religions was the reason for the gospel then Jesus would not have sent out His disciples to make the world followers of Him.

If I have offended you by my comments then I am sorry you are offended. The deity of Jesus the Christ is as clear to me as it is in scripture. With that clarity it would be wrong for me to say that there is hope without Jesus. You might get through this life without Him, but you certainly won't get through the next. If you have not met Jesus it's because you don't want to. He gave an invitation out when He said in -:

Revelations 3v20
Look, I'm standing at the door and knocking. If anyone listens to my voice and opens the door I'll come in and we'll eat together.

Do you want to accept His invitation? That's *WHERE THE RUBBER MEETS THE ROAD*.

Of the Ten Commandments the first two show us how important Father really is to us. We are not left with any doubt as to what the Lord thinks regarding mockers -:

Gal. 6v7
Make no mistake about this; You can never make a fool out of God. Whatever you plant is what you'll harvest.

He also gives us a warning in-:

1 John5v21
Dear children guard yourselves from false Gods.

* Read;- *Concise Guide to Today's Religions* by Josh McDowell & Don Stewart

What price do we pay in a society that can accommodate tolerance in every field? The minorities become a majority in a culture that refuses to be directed on life's paths. Can we not learn that the human is never satisfied with guide line perimeters. He will always push, like a child testing it's parents boundaries. Man is not concerned if the gains are to his long term benifit, only the present matters. The instant now has taken the seat of patience, with morality being exchanged for progressivness in this live and let live (as long as it does not effect me) society.

Clergy dispute and argue about the cornerstones of salvation. Watering down and diluting beliefs and doctrines just to accommodate modern man's thoughts on spiritual life. Guardians of the faith declare that homage has to be given to other religions, thus moving aside Christian structure to make way for world-wide doctrines. It would be so easy, under the name of peace to accept their ways. Should we not be mending the division that runs through Christian churches instead of inviting other Gods into His places of worship? The gaps created by our own divisions drive leaders to reach out, not with the gospel, but with human intent. Other doctrines and false religions press in from all sides, each offering another aspect or insight from their beliefs. They seem happy to be allowed to preach that the heart of man will be contented if he has any higher power sitting there. Is the heart of man not reserved for the Christ? The only God to have died for His children. Meanwhile wolves from our own flocks, under the flag of unity, give credibility to them and become a part of the ungodly circle of mockers. If we couple this with the contempt of an atheistic media we find ourselves in a pot of mongrel soup. It is time to be separate. Separate in our ways to Him but fully embracing the unbeliever of every persuasion.

Did Jesus not say "I am the way the truth and the life, no one comes to the Father except through me." He also looked at scriptural leaders of the day, and called them a "brood of vipers" because of their unbelief in Him. Is His word not clear when it is said in-:

Acts 4v12
No one else can save us. Indeed, we can be saved only by the power of the one named Jesus and not by any other person.

We can't forget that our God will not share His deity or worship with any one.

Now is the time to come together in unity as Christians and share our Lords Love and Living Faith with the followers of worldly religions. His love abounds for them just as much, if not more, as it does for us. Did He not leave the ninety nine to go and get the one? He is the Creator and we are the created beings. He want's to use to restore His beloved children. So let us stick steadfast to His truth by not compromising, thus giving credence to the ungodly circle of mockers. The harvest is ready and our Lord wants to gather in His lambs and sheep.

That's *WHERE THE RUBBER MEETS THE ROAD.*

Secret Touch

Let me reach you Lord and take You to me
Just like Jesus when we are one I am free
Saturated grace with mercy and gifts as such
Oh how I need your peaceful and secret touch

-Chorus-

You have taken a captured and broken heart
For what reason I may not understand
You have taken a captured and broken heart
To be moulded and orchestrated by a loving hand

What words can I say to so noble a King
What kind of melody can I make music sing
What kind of dance would please my eternal Father
What can be shown when in your arms you gather

-Chorus-

I move aside Lord and let you draw near
Casting away heaviness, pain and worldly fear
Holy Spirit move my being with purity I desire
Kindle Your presence that once was a fire

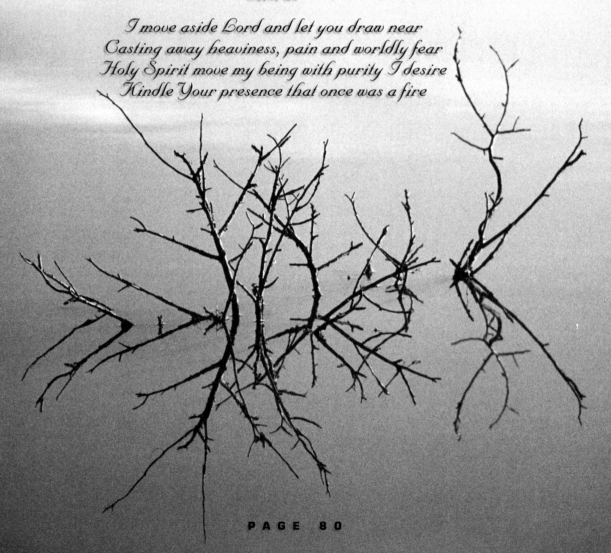

WAIT 'N WATCH

My size forty waist did not tell lies. I had put on weight. I was encouraged to go to one of those "Eat less Points" classes that has a clientele mostly made up of women. To say I was embarrassed would be to understate the word "embarrassed". There I sat after being weighed, knowing that if I had weighed my new weight I would need to go out and start buying 42-44 inch trousers. The evidence was there before me as I listened to the ten point programme. Ladies testified that they had done well that week and the ones who hadn't were encouraged to do better for the next. I was so glad to get away after the meeting and find that all my forty inch waist trousers still fitted me.

I was that relieved to get the experience over with that I even cut back my own eating habits (with the help of the Lord of course). I got a follow up letter (in rhyme) welcoming me to the group. I thought "that's nice". Then after a week I got another (in rhyme) telling me I need not stay a 42-44 waster (or is that waister)? Anyway I composed the wee ode below with a tongue in cheek sense of humour. Seriously though, my Lord and Saviour is interested in everything I do. That includes trying to loose weight. He has built in warning signs like getting fat, becoming breathless, having a sore back, always feeling tired, etc. To us fatties there is hope, as long as I can take the doughnut out of my heart, for my heart belongs to Jesus. Watch this space.

"WATCH 'N WEIGHT"

Wit a **surprize** wae tears in mha **eyes** ye hiv rote notes tae me **twice**
Ah don't want tae go **back** coz gulability ah **lack** bit yer wee jester wiz **nice**
The wate ah'v on **remishion** mite cost ye **comishon** bit ah'l dae this wee thing ma **sel**
It'z a **shame** thit finance iz the **game** az the Wate Watchers coffers get fat an **swell**
Bit thanks fur the **kerd** az tae mha shape ye **infered**, ah thot it wiz really really **funny**
A good biznis **ploy** fur an overwate **boy** who diznay want tae gei ye eny mer **muney**

Fondest Regards

Pat

Just a wee poem that came as I was trying to work out reality. It was probably inspired by someone who said to me "Yoor no reel."

John 1v1-5
In the beginning the Word already existed. The Word was with God, and the Word was God. He was already with God in the beginning. Everything came into existence through Him. Not one thing that existed was made without Him. He was the source of life, and that life was the light for humanity. The light shines in the dark, and the dark has never extinguished it.

GETTING REAL

A Christian sailor was shipwrecked and as he bobbed about in the sea a helicopter appeared. The winchman told the Christian to get hold of the line. The Christian replied "It's OK I am waiting on the Lord to rescue me." One hour latter a passing ship drew up beside him and offered to bring him aboard. "Thanks but No. I am waiting on the Lord to rescue me." A few hours later a submarine rose from the depths and threw him a life line. "I don't need it" said the Christian "I am waiting on the Lord's rescue."

After a day in the water he drowned. When he met the Lord he said "Lord my faith was large enough, why did you not rescue me?" Father smiled at him and said "My son I sent a helicopter a boat and a submarine to get you."

REALITY

what is reality in this day that we live
being wealthy in an nation unable to give
we pamper and plan our short term goals
while forgetting about man and their eternal souls

reality is not here and now, it doesn't have a floor or a ceiling
it can't touch the furthest star, or be a miraculous healing
it won't come into force at death, nor at the birth of a baby
it doesn't stamp it's authority on an intention, a promise or a maybe

reality is truth eternal, an everlasting voice
not designed to boss you about but to give you freedom for choice
it's the alpha the omega the only source of being
a god who is all life all love all caring and all seeing

for reality goes even further than this
it's an eternity for worship that no one should miss
in this feat, what father has done
is to incorporate earth's time scale for the glory of his son

six days to make, six days to mold
a universe so large, that our minds can't hold
creation was ordained and spoken out by him
it came into being, unspoiled without blemish or sin

no mind can fathom the depth or the riches of his love
the continuous out pouring , from his godly throne above
so reality always was, always is and always shall be
it is the god father whose heart is geared towards me

reality is also a ransom that's been paid in full
removing bond's from a satanic realm and it's earthly rule
it has no beginning and there is no end
when he returns, in his presence, eternal reality we will spend

CRUCIFIED

Knowing all, as he walked tall, asking the mob who it was that was wanted
Answering him "The man without sin, Jesus the Nazarene" they taunted,
"I am here" came the words, without fear, as they backed away and fell to the ground,
"If you came for me, set the others free" His authority was louder than sound.

"I lost none whom Father gave to the Son" words for me and you.
Prophesy complete in a verbal feat with RHEMA tested plain and true.
Out came a sword to protect his Lord, Simon Peter drew back and struck with steel.
Malchus' ear was cut so severe, but a touch from the healer did amputation heal.

"Put your sword away, is this not my day to drink from my Fathers cup"
"I won't be denied, by the spirits that hide, my destiny will now I sup"
Bound so tight, without a fight, the Roman soldiers arrested Jesus at pace,
Guards did beat with fists and feet as they pulled the beard from his face.

Insulting behaviour covered the Saviour, as taunts rose from the pit of hell,
"For one man to die would be a human high" Caiaphas a salvation prediction did tell,
A fire was lit where Peter did sit "You are one of His followers and a servant"
Looking at the girl, his head did swirl, his denial was quick and fervent.

Later on, some had gone, another voice declared "You are one of them too"
In a sweat from authority threat the rock's outburst was duplicated, as rejection grew,
More than an hour his mouth tasted sour, as a Galilean he was pointed to yet again
"I do not know what you are trying to sow" from rejecting his Lord he could not refrain.

With three defections sowed, the dawn rooster crowed, into Jesus' eyes his look leapt,
Grieved with despair, without any repair, tears hot with pain, Peter wept.
Not to stay, he went away, as the blindfold with insults on his master began to unfold,
Showing no disgrace they punched the face of a man whose heart was as pure as gold.

Accused, physically abused, Jesus saw Barabbus released according to Jewish law,
Then He was stripped and so severely whipped that his back revealed white bones raw.
Shouts of "Long live the King" with slaps that did sting, they threw on the cloak of red,
Branches of thorn were woven in scorn and pushed ever so deep into his head.

Going outside, Pilot could not hide, as he called "Look here is the man,"
"Crucify" came the mobs reply as they imparted fear into the Governor's release plan.
Before the Passover feast, Emmanuael was released into hands of a dark plot agreed.
With soldiers all around, Simon of Cyrene was found to carry the cross that freed.

With Golgotha ahead, he turned and said "Women of Jerusalem don't you cry for me"
Two men of theft hung to his right and his left, as Jesus was nailed to the cursed tree.
"Father forgive them" was the call for one and all, as the dice tumbled for his cloak.
With a vinegar sponge a soldier did lunge as "I'm thirsty" from his lips words broke.

At noon, darkness came so soon, when the suns rays refused to glow
Every demonic being at Calvery were seeing, their defeat at an open public show
Pressing down like a dark gown separated from Abba but not his goal
"I am not mistaken for I am forsaken, my Father's presence has left my soul"

"It is finished" he said, with a bowed head, as he gave up his spirit broken and crushed
The curtain was split like a sword slit, as the last of his life's blood had gushed
Taken away to be buried that day, the notice in languages read "King of the Jews"
The pain endured, that we may have life ensured, he paid all of mans debts and dues

The best that I can give, in the world I live, is to believe in Him who was given
Repent of the past, and walk the path that is cast, and to Him go on living.
I don't understand for my mind can't expand, but I'm going to love him best I can
There is nothing I can do, except tell maybe you, that He is God's eternal plan

This was the first song I wrote. After a luke-warm glare (really silent criticism), a relative made a funny and patronising comment about not giving up the day job. It got shelved. I now release it into your care.

John 3v16
God loved the world this way; He gave His only Son so that everyone who believes in Him will not die but have eternal life.

WILLING SACRIFICE

Early in my Christian walk we had an outreach team from Canada who visited us to help evangelise in Drumchapel. One of the group told me of this story.

A Christian summer log camp in the States was visited by one of the above group. Seeing as there were hundreds attending this break, the camp had it's own butcher along with livestock. When it came time to slaughter a pig, there was such a commotion. The pig fought, kicked and squealed. It tried to bite as it looked for an escape. It struggled and wriggled and it took a while for the pig to be finally put down. A lamb was next to be slaughtered. There was no commotion like the one from the pig. No bleating or biting, it went silently and lay in the hands of the slaughterman and within a couple of minutes it was over.

I took so much from this story. I was like the pig, refusing to put my life down for the Lord. Kicking and fighting His love, running away from His prompting. Yet there He was, the King of Kings putting His life down for me without even a word of dissent. I will allow you to think about it.

Dali's Christ of St John of the Cross.
Glasgow Museums-:
The St Mungo Museum of Reliious Life & Art

HE HUNG ALONE THAT DAY

Prepared to die for you and I
That's the reasons why
He hung alone that day

No cries of pain as He was slain
No one thought that He would reign
As he hung alone that day

"Father please forgive them, they don't know what they do
As I freely give my life I now commit them unto You"
As I hang alone this day

Separated from Father, no more He could take
"My God why have you forsaken me"
Surely it was for mankind's sake
As He hung alone that day

No bones were broken, no blood was left
With a call that shook the earth "It is finished" is what He said
As He hung alone that day

As death crept over Him, and darkness was all around
Who knew this man would rise again
And be so easily found
As He hung alone that day

For the first time in eternity, through sin there was a break
Father, Son and Holy Ghost separated for my sake
As He hung alone that day

Satan's plans are defeated, no more prey can he infect
Nor steal kill and destroy because Jesus died to protect
When He hung alone that day

He gave us life through His death, the shedding of His blood
No more chains or bondage now or crawling in the mud
As He hung alone that day

The love for you and I, is not dependent on the season
It's an agape eternal love the Trinity's oneness was the reason
That He hung alone that day

It's not hard to see where we struggle with the Word of God. We have the Word in black and white yet we allow the grey matter between our ears to become a battle ground for the devil to conduct his war. We know the truths of the Word while we become entrapped by guilt and condemnation. I wrote the next rhyme at a time when I struggled with the above title and constantly brought my failings to Father even though the truths below are self explanatory -:

Romans 3v23-24
Because all people have sinned, they have fallen short of God's glory.
They receive God's approval freely by an act of kindness (grace)
through the price Christ Jesus paid to set us free
(from sin).

Was I thinking that His sacrifice did not cover the sins that I commit? Surely not, but the mind can be very persuasive when it comes to self condemnation. Does it not say in-:

Rom. 8v1
Therefore, there is now no condemnation for those who are in Christ Jesus. NIV

So apparently I was being conned by condemnation. That is only until we read-:

Ps. 103v12
As far east is from west that is how far He has removed our rebellious acts from Himself.

The wonderful thing about this little gem is that the writer did not write "as far North was to South" The reason being that if I continue to walk northward I would finally come to the south. On the other hand if I walk Eastward I never come to the West. Our Father chooses not to remember our sins and yet we hold on to them like a type of penance giving the enemy a foothold to condemn. I know you all probably have had the revelation of this but it is a little nugget that helped me.

So on this page we have the Word and in the poem we have the feelings. Feelings that have a bedrock of insecurity guilt and sin. On this bedrock Satan plants his seed. The only way to be forgiven is to say sorry. Feelings against scripture are common but there is only one winner. Feelings will pass away but His Word is for ever-:

Mark 13v31
The earth and the heavens will disappear, but my words will never disappear.

REPETITIOUS REPENTING

Repetitious Repenting encircles and hides the habit of sin
Ashamed to ask for mercy so that once again I can begin
Separation from Father is far from thought when transgression starts to kick
Even a check in the heart is suppressed as my being takes the path I pick

The sin runs its course leaving me a shell empty depressed and void
Oh how I miss His presence His peace and being totally overjoyed
My wages have been paid in and there is only one withdrawal to make
I'm heading in the wrong direction I'm a failure a sinner and a fake

I told Him I loved Him and His ways I would follow for ever through
How can I expect Him to believe me that I will from now on be true
The pain and the parting from my Lord is too big a burden to hold
Lord forgive me and my weakness to sin and restore me to the fold

I am sorry for rejecting all Your love from the terrible Calvary pain
Draw me closer Lord that I may remember Your Son's blood gain
Forgive me as You forgave David a man after Your own heart
Forgive me Lord as I repent being determined to make a new start

I can't live without Your presence in a world destitute in love
I won't function without Your direction or prodding from above
I don't want to be here if by Your hand I can't walk
I need the blood of Jesus and an ear to hear when You talk

So forgive me my Father as to the Christ's blood I plead
My sin was stuck firmly to the tree on that day they made Him bleed
I repent of transgression and the repetition that holds together as one
He is my Saviour, my Lord and in Him my cleansing has once again begun

Going Round in Circles...

I told him to turn right at the round-about an hour ago

NEVER

Never have I seen a fire that does not smoulder or smoke
Never have I seen anger that does not rile or provoke
Never have I seen a rainbow minus a shower or squall
Never have I seen a vase break without a tumble or fall

Never have I seen a sea that does not ebb and flow
Never have I seen a day break when darkness does not go
Never have I seen bitterness that does not burrow and bite deep
Never have I seen an insomniac who can command sleep

Never have I seen a yacht moving without wind in it's sails
Never have I seen harmony when bickering prevails
Never have I seen a divorce without some regret or pain
Never have I seen a peaceful mind in a person of the insane

Never have I seen man's desire to reject the habit to point or accuse
Never have I seen a rich man get more finance to then refuse
Never have I seen the poor and sick with joy in abundance galore
Never have I seen the orphan without a rejection pain that's sore

Never have I seen love without actions being attached
Never have I seen forgiveness without memory being detached
Never have I seen a church fall with forgiveness and care
Never have I seen freedom in a heart when God's presence is not there

Never have I seen a covenant piled up and stacked in mankind's favour
Never have I seen souls healed and prisoners free because of a Saviour
Never have I seen a contract without a penalty or a small print code
Never have I seen salvation needing only a verbal repentance mode

Never have I seen a Son so perfect and yet despised and rejected
Never have I seen a sacrifice so terrible but holy and lovely infected
Never have I seen a Father who gave so much to benefit human ways
Never have I seen condemnation rejected unless in men's hearts He stays

This was a song inspired by the Bishop of York when he proclaimed that "The Virgin Birth didn't matter." Over the years we have heard many basic truth's being watered down and undermined by leaders who really should know better. I still feel strongly opposed to any leader, or person, coming against the basic truths of Christianity. God's word is there for all and all should have the chance to read and hear it undiluted of it's content. If then the reader or the hearer decides it's not for them they at least will have had the full story of Father's Love, Grace, Mercy and POWER

2 Tim. 3v13
But evil people and phoney preachers will go from bad to worse as they mislead people and are themselves misled.

YOU ARE MY LORD

Confusion abounds around at every wind of change
Followers have lost their ground and make your teaching strange
One denies your birth another denies your deity
How can they say they are one and in unity

CHORUS
You are my God you are the Holy One
You are my Lord you are the risen Son

They all deny you were the chosen Lamb
Putting aside the Trinity's Oneness and eternal plan
Why can't they see the new life you give for free
All they have to do is turn things back to you

CHORUS

I heard things said in my quest for the truth
But the way you died gave our relationship no excuse
Standing that night with tears falling free
You touched my heart in a way that I could see

CHORUS

"I am the way", were the words you used that day
Setting me apart from life going astray
I know you Jesus I know you as my Lord
Holy Spirit and Father you are my God

CHORUS

As I walk you show me Father's love
From day to day guiding me from above
Prepared to reveal your love for me was real
It's now I see what happened on that tree

CHORUS

Options

Inspiration of the heart surpasses the human mind
It tends to bypass logic using emotions signed
Life lessons bring maturity to both thought and deed
Giving man's soul a hunger that only God can feed

The will has to submit and yield to let the flow begin
No place for darkened condemnation nor unrepented sin
In comes the light of the world so peacefully formed
The battle's over as the gates of hell have been stormed

Man's ways are due to end as eternity gathers around
Adam to Jesus we were informed by every prophetic sound
A submitted spirit can now house the King of the biblical story
So are you alert for His arrival on the greatest day of Glory

The sky rolls back with conclusion sealed on the eternal clock
Sweeping aside the devil He gathers and collects His free-willed flock
Oh the Majesty and Mercy from One so Mighty and Great
Separating the sheep from the goats He directs through Heaven's gate

There will be a wailing and gnashing of teeth like never heard before
But man has the chance now as Jesus knocks at the heart's door
Opposition to human independence? Do you do your own thing?
Lucifer told Adam he didn't need God but that was the eternal sting

So I guess it's up to us when we weigh up all the options of life
Man's way or God's way to separate like cutting cake with a knife
Deciding isn't hard but consequences will await its timely prize
Choose right and escape the tears of regret that will surely swamp your eyes

Hiv ye ever dun sumthin ye didnay want tae dae
Dain drugs dain drink goat involved in sexual play
Hiz yer violint actions or wurds cauzed ye tae feel doon
Wishin ye hidnay dun it bit like the roond a boot ye go roon an roon

D'ye get wee twinjiz at yer reactshons wishin ye'd dun bettir
Crinjin tae yersel like wen ye get a summins ora wee red det lettir
Shoutin an acuzin tae hooz nearest coz they ur always in the rang
Bit inside ye desire tae get it rite peecfuly an no wae a soor tastin tang

An wit aboot the lies an truths thit's used twistin them aw the gether fur gain
Hopin we kin remember wit wiz wit withoot oor heeds gon insane
We tipple wen wi get tae the boatim o the barrel coz nuthin effects wit we feel
Hivin used aw family an friends its ther luv an emoshons thit we steel

Intenshins stie intenshins until a change or a deed iz intraduced
We need tae move intae another geer jist tae get oor feet 'n heed loosed
"Next time" promises quench an dilute the pains o gilt an regret
Remorsefuly "Bein sorry" soon subsides coz oor acshons it's met

Manz goat two natures ur ye surprised thit thats wit the bible sayz
A curupt nature alang wie a spiritual wan tae acumpany him throo hiz dayz
Its like gon intae a mental war in sum o the disishons he try's tae make
"Aye ah wul, No a wulnay", he jist diznay want tae make another mistake

Noo thit we know thit we hiv two kinds o nature in oor bein
A human side demandin an weak thit hooses oor spirit jenraly unseen
Wan nature we goat fae Adam an wan we goat fae God
Gie yersel a shake an allow yer brain tae cum oot o the wurlds conformin pod*

Oor flesh wull return tae the durt an oor spirit goes before the wan hoo givz
*Iclaiziasties makes this clear and withoot a dout He'z the God hoo livz
So how cum ah canny dae wit a want tae an ah dae the things ah want tae bin
The mistery Paul rites in *Romins states oor humin nature is curupt an selt oot tae sin

Don't think fur a minut thit the battle goin oan inside iz novul ur new
Coz the wurdz o life ur fur aw mankind an no jist the chosin few
Ur ye redy fur a wee revelashon wurds o life able tae open yir mind
Well get intae *Galashons an *Ifeeshinz an aw the abuv info yoo'l find

Ye mite ask, how cum this Faithir God hiz goat aw oor good in His hart
Bit if we new wit He new an luved like He luved then we wid never be apart
Ah jist beleev He luvs uz espeshally wen we cry fae oor sin an stain
He picks uz up He moves uz on He comforts an heels oor deepist pain

*Romans 12v2 *ECCLESIASTES 12v7 *ROMANS 7v14-25 *GALATIANS 5v16-25 *EPHESIANS 2v1-10

THANK YOU LORD

Thank You for the way you have made me giving me a heart to care
Thank You for your Spirit within making me ever so rare
Thank You for choosing me and setting me aside
Thank You for the revelation of your being at a time I wanted to hide
Thank You for the free will to decide between flesh and spirit
Thank You for the grace and mercy and love without limit
Thank You for your protection in all ways of my walk
Thank You for your presence when about you I talk
Thank You for every gift and even the breath I take
Thank You for my children, custom built for my sake
Thank You for the sun the hail the rain and the snow
Thank You for todays blessings when into the world I go
Thank You when I'm down low or in the depth of despair
Thank You for your understanding when with love my heart You repair
Thank You when I'm mocked or undermined in any kind of way
Thank You that in your time You will defend me with love to repay
Thank You for being there when things are sad or unreal
Thank You for your affections no matter how I feel
Thank You for your forgiveness when every time I fall
Thank You for your timing when You answer my cry or call
Thank You for your comfort when things get tight or really rough
Thank You for the path in the swamp or the hard rocky stuff
Thank You for the plans and goals that still lie ahead
Thank You that you have a place reserved for me for when I'm dead
Thank You being dead means being free and alive with you
Thank You for the heavenly plan that You will carry out and see through
Thank You that You accept that all I am is a child who believes
Thank You for the gift of faith that helps me to my knees
Thank You for your hand when I have no where to run
Thank You for the Word that became flesh I know He's your Son
Thank You for your Spirit that makes up the Trinity's three
Thank You that between yourselves you set this sinner free
Thank You for all my failures because it's then I know your strength
Thank You for the eternal sacrifice when you went full length

1 Thes. 5v18:
Whatever happens, give thanks, because it is God's will in Christ Jesus
that you do this.

A thankful heart is the parent of all virtues.
                    Cicero

Short and sweet
An oral treat
To poesy steer
Keeping it clear

No debris dross
With words gross
Forget verbal rocks
From personal talks

Coming or going
To-ing or fro-ing
Death will steal
Life not real

Existence of hits
Drugged grief pits
Only one chance
Break the trance

A story fine
On spiritual line
Dark heart unseen
Open to clean

Escape sin's wrath
Thin narrow path
Just one choice
The eternal voice

Jesus He wept
Sin's rejection swept
Saviour then died
Man was revived

Repented open heart
New reality start
The Holy Spirit
Grace without limit

Children at base
Father's Holy face
Together as one
Like trinity's Son

WELL ?

What can I say to you reader who does not know the Lord? Can I convince you with words that will sweep you into the Kingdom? Can I convince you with wit or charm? The answer is surely "No." What I do know and testify to you is that He (Jesus) is not far from you. By the power of the Holy Spirit you can meet Him right now. Please forgive me for being so abrupt but if it takes my bad manners to entice you to talk to my Saviour in the quietness of your heart then my abruptness is irrelevant.

This world is designed for you to turn your back on Him who gave His back for us. He gave His life to set us free from broken hearts and loose the chains and bondage of an ancient serpent who is destined to be locked away for ever. Soften your heart this day and open the lock on your heart that the King of Glory may come in.

Only three things you need to know.

FIRST, you must know that you are a sinner and that you are lost.

Nearly three thousand years ago the prophet Isaiah recorded:

> **Isaiah 53v6**
> *WE have all strayed like sheep.*
> *Each one of us has turned to go his own way, and the Lord has laid ALL our sins on Him.*

Then Paul says in Romans eight hundred years later:

> **Romans 3v23**
> *Because all people have sinned, they have fallen short of God's glory.*

I do not know what you think of God but the above two scriptures tell us where we stand in His eyes.

SECOND, there is nothing I can do to save myself.

> **Titus 3v5**
> *He saved us, but not because of anything we had done to gain His approval. Instead, because of His mercy He saved us through the washing in which the Holy Spirit gives us new birth and renewal.*

Again in Ephesians Paul writes:

> **Eph. 29**
> *God saved you through faith as an act of kindness. You had nothing to do with it. Being saved is a gift from God. It's not the result of anything you have done, so no one can brag about it.*

Doing wee good things does not wash away the original stain we inherited from Adam. We cannot do a thing except BELIEVE that He has already done it and only He has the authority to release us. Self -salvation is impossible.

THIRD, you must know that Jesus Christ and Him alone can save you. Matthew testifies in:

> **Matt. 1v21**
> *She will give birth to a son, and you will name him Jesus (He Saves), because he will save his people from their sins.*

He then again writes in:

> ### Acts 4v12
> *No one else can save us. Indeed, we can be saved only by the power of the one named Jesus and not by any other person.*

So Matthew gives it to us as it is. Mohammed, Confucius, Buddha, Catholic, Protestant, Greek Orthodox, Judaism do not have the authority to save. Neither do ceremonies, pilgrimages, cults nor deeds of merit. Thank God that there is one who has the authority and the power and that one is the Christ, Jesus Christ. Will you believe?

The mystery is revealed.

Dear reader there is no mystery involved. To receive the living God into your life is as plain as the nose on your face. John the favourite disciple records in:

> ### John 1v12
> *However, he gave the right to become God's children to every one who believed in him.*

So here is the prayer:

> *Lord, today I stand before you.*
> *I know that I am a sinner and I turn from those sins.*
> *I ask for your forgiveness.*
> *I believe that you were sent to die for me*
> *that I might come to you today and give you my life.*
> *I believe that you rose from the dead.*
> *I give you my heart and my life*
> *and I ask that you come into my life today.*
> *I pray for the baptism in the Holy Spirit.*

Thank you so much for reading this book. I don't know what kind of effect it has had on you. What I do know is that nothing I have written will sustain you in your walk nor will it sweep you into the Kingdom. What I do know is that if you trust Him the way I have (by His grace) then I will see you in eternity.